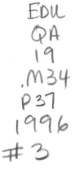

D1429975

GRADES 5-6

...the Super Source™
Pattern Blocks

Cuisenaire Company of America, Inc.
White Plains, NY

Cuisenaire extends its warmest thanks to the many teachers and students across the country who helped ensure the success of the Super Source™ series by participating in the outlining, writing, and field testing of the materials.

Project Director: Judith Adams
Managing Editor: Doris Hirschhorn
Editorial Team: John Nelson, Deborah J. Slade, Harriet Slonim
Field Test Coordinator: Laurie Verdeschi

Design Manager: Phyllis Aycock
Text Design: Amy Berger, Tracey Munz
Line Art and Production: Joan Lee, Fiona Santoianni
Cover Design: Michael Muldoon
Illustrations: Rebecca Thornburgh

1 2 3 4 5 - 00 - 99 98 97 96

...the Super Source™

Table of Contents

Using the Super Source™

The Super Source™ is a series of books, each of which contains a collection of activities to use with a specific math manipulative. Driving **the Super Source**™ is Cuisenaire's conviction that children construct their own understandings through rich, hands-on mathematical experiences. Although the activities in each book are written for a specific grade range, they all connect to the core of mathematics learning that is important to every K-6 child. Thus, the material in many activities can easily be refocused for children at other grade levels. Because the activities are not arranged sequentially, children can work on any activity at any time.

The lessons in **the Super Source**™ all follow a basic structure consistent with the vision of mathematics teaching described in the *Curriculum and Evaluation Standards for School Mathematics* published by the National Council of Teachers of Mathematics.

All of the activities in this series involve Problem Solving, Communication, Reasoning, and Mathematical Connections—the first four NCTM Standards. Each activity also focuses on one or more of the following curriculum strands: Number, Geometry, Measurement, Patterns/Functions, Probability/Statistics, Logic.

HOW LESSONS ARE ORGANIZED

At the beginning of each lesson, you will find, to the right of the title, both the major curriculum strands to which the lesson relates and the particular topics that children will work with. Each lesson has three main sections. The first, GETTING READY, offers an *Overview*, which states what children will be doing, and why, and provides a list of "What You'll Need." Specific numbers of Pattern Blocks are suggested on this list but can be adjusted as the needs of your specific situation dictate. Before an activity, blocks can be counted out and placed in containers or self-sealing plastic bags for easy distribution. When crayons are called for, it is understood that their colors are those that match the Pattern Blocks and that markers may be used in place of crayons. Blackline masters that are provided for your convenience at the back of the book are also referenced on this materials list. Paper, pencils, scissors, tape, and materials for making charts, which may be necessary in certain activities, are usually not.

Although overhead Pattern Blocks are always listed in "What You'll Need" as optional, these materials are highly effective when you want to demonstrate the use of Pattern Blocks. As you move blocks on the screen, children can work with the same materials at their seats. If overhead Pattern Blocks are not available, you may want to make and use transparencies of the Pattern Block shapes (see page 91). Children can also use the overhead Pattern Blocks and/or a transparency of the triangle paper to present their work to other members of their group or to the class.

The second section, THE ACTIVITY, first presents a possible scenario for *Introducing* the children to the activity. The aim of this brief introduction is to help you give children the tools they will need to investigate independently. However, care has been taken to avoid undercutting the activity itself. Since these investigations are designed to enable children to increase their own mathematical power, the idea is to set the stage but not steal the show! The heart of the lesson, *On Their Own*, is found in a box at the top of the second page of each lesson. Here, rich problems stimulate many different problem-solving approaches and lead to a variety of solutions. These hands-on explorations have the potential for bringing children to new mathematical ideas and deepening skills.

On Their Own is intended as a stand-alone activity for children to explore with a partner or in a small group. Be sure to make the needed directions clearly visible. You may want to write them on the chalkboard or on an overhead or present them either on reusable cards or paper. For children who may have difficulty reading the directions, you can read them aloud or make sure that at least one "reader" is in each group.

The last part of this second section, *The Bigger Picture*, gives suggestions for how children can share their work and their thinking and make mathematical connections. Class charts and children's recorded work provide a springboard for discussion. Under "Thinking and Sharing," there are several prompts that you can use to promote discussion. Children will not be able to respond to these prompts with one-word answers. Instead, the prompts encourage children to describe what they notice, tell how they found their results, and give the reasoning behind their answers. Thus children learn to verify their own results rather than relying on the teacher to determine if an answer is "right" or "wrong." Though the class discussion might immediately follow the investigation, it is important not to cut the activity short by having a class discussion too soon.

The Bigger Picture often includes a suggestion for a "Writing" (or drawing) assignment. This is meant to help children process what they have just been doing. You might want to use these ideas as a focus for daily or weekly entries in a math journal that each child keeps.

1. The Blue rombus has The same area as The square. 2. The white rombus is half the hight of The orange

From: *Comparing Area*

2. What did you look for to find an equilateral shape. I look for sides that are the same. It also helps to see if they are symetrical

From: *Reach Into the Bag*

The Bigger Picture always ends with ideas for "Extending the Activity." Extensions take the essence of the main activity and either alter or extend its parameters. These activities are well used with a class that becomes deeply involved in the primary activity or for children who finish before the others. In any case, it is probably a good idea to expose the entire class to the possibility of, and the results from, such extensions.

The third and final section of the lesson is TEACHER TALK. Here, in *Where's the Mathematics?*, you can gain insight into the underlying mathematics of the activity and discover some of the strategies children are apt to use as they work. Solutions are also given— when such are necessary and/or helpful. Because *Where's the Mathematics?* provides a view of what may happen in the lesson as well as the underlying mathematical potential that may grow out of it, this may be the section that you want to read before presenting the activity to children.

USING THE ACTIVITIES

The Super Source™ has been designed to fit into the variety of classroom environments in which it will be used. These range from a completely manipulative-based classroom to one in which manipulatives are just beginning to play a part. You may choose to use some activities in **the Super Source**™ in the way set forth in each lesson (introducing an activity to the whole class, then breaking the class up into groups that all work on the same task, and so forth). You will then be able to circulate among the groups as they work to observe and perhaps comment on each child's work. This approach requires a full classroom set of materials but allows you to concentrate on the variety of ways that children respond to a given activity.

Alternatively, you may wish to make two or three related activities available to different groups of children at the same time. You may even wish to use different manipulatives to explore the same mathematical concept. (Geoboards and Tangrams, for example, can be used to teach some of the same geometric principles as Pattern Blocks.) This approach does not require full classroom sets of a particular manipulative. It also permits greater adaptation of materials to individual children's needs and/or preferences.

If children are comfortable working independently, you might want to set up a "menu"— that is, set out a number of related activities from which children can choose. Children should be encouraged to write about their experiences with these independent activities.

However you choose to use **the Super Source**™ activities, it would be wise to allow time for several groups or the entire class to share their experiences. The dynamics of this type of interaction, where children share not only solutions and strategies but also feelings and intuitions, is the basis of continued mathematical growth. It allows children who are beginning to form a mathematical structure to clarify it and those who have mastered just isolated concepts to begin to see how these concepts might fit together.

Again, both the individual teaching style and combined learning styles of the children should dictate the specific method of utilizing **the Super Source**™ lessons. At first sight, some activities may appear too difficult for some of your children, and you may find yourself tempted to actually "teach" by modeling exactly how an activity can lead to a particular learning outcome. If you do this, you rob children of the chance to try the activity in whatever way they can. As long as children have a way to begin an investigation, give them time and opportunity to see it through. Instead of making assumptions about what children will or won't do, watch and listen. The excitement and challenge of the activity—as well as the chance to work cooperatively—may bring out abilities in children that will surprise you.

If you are convinced, however, that an activity does not suit your students, adjust it, by all means. You may want to change the language, either by simplifying it or by referring to specific vocabulary that you and your children already use and are comfortable with. On the other hand, if you suspect that an activity isn't challenging enough, you may want to read through the activity extensions for a variation that you can give children instead.

RECORDING

Although the direct process of working with Pattern Blocks is a valuable one, it is afterward, when children look at, compare, share, and think about their constructions, that an activity yields its greatest rewards. However, because Pattern Block designs can't always be left intact for very long, children need an effective way to record their work. To this end, at the back of this book recording paper is provided for reproduction. The "What You'll Need" listing at the beginning of each lesson often specifies the kind of recording paper to use. For example, in an activity where children are working with only the yellow, red, blue, and green Pattern Blocks, they can duplicate their work or trace the Pattern Block pieces on the Pattern Block triangle paper found on page 90.

From: *Find All the Perimeters*

From: *Fraction Puzzles*

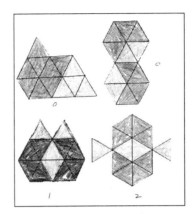

From: *Looking for Symmetry*

When they also work with the orange and/or tan Pattern Blocks, children need a plain piece of recording paper, since these Pattern Block pieces don't fit neatly onto the triangle paper.

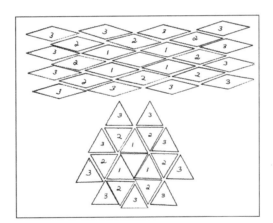

From: *Surround*

In this latter case, the children will have to find a way to transfer their Pattern Block designs. They might choose to trace each Pattern Block piece in the design onto the plain paper or to use a Pattern Block template to reproduce each piece in the design. Templates of the exact size and shape of the Pattern Blocks can be bought or made from plastic coffee-can lids.

When young children explore Pattern Blocks, they are likely to use up every available block in making a huge pattern. This makes the pattern daunting to copy. Such patterns may be recorded using cutouts of the Pattern Block shapes (see page 91). Children can color the shapes and paste them in place on white paper.

Another interesting way to "freeze" a Pattern Block design is to create it using a software piece, such as *Shape Up!*, and then get a printout. Children can use a classroom or resource-room computer if it is available or, where possible, extend the activity into a home assignment by utilizing their home computers.

Recording involves more than copying the designs. Writing, drawing, and making charts and tables are also ways to record. By creating a table of data gathered in the course of their investigations, children are able to draw conclusions and look for patterns. When children write or draw, either in their group or later by themselves, they are clarifying their understanding of their recent mathematical experience.

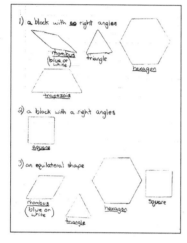

From: *Reach Into the Bag*

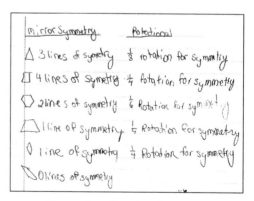

From: *How Many Can Sit?*

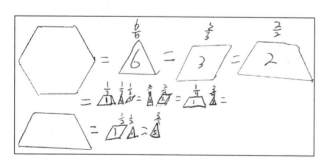

From: *What's My Value?*

From: *Looking for Symmetry*

With a roomful of children busily engaged in their investigations, it is not easy for a teacher to keep track of how individual children are working. Having tangible material to gather and examine when the time is right will help you to keep in close touch with each child's learning.

Exploring Pattern Blocks

A set of Pattern Blocks consists of blocks in six geometric, color-coded shapes, referred to as: green triangles, orange squares, blue parallelograms, tan rhombuses, red trapezoids, and yellow hexagons. The relationships among the side measures and among the angle measures make it very easy to fit the blocks together to make tiling patterns which completely cover a flat surface. The blocks are designed so that all the sides of the shapes are 1 inch except the longer side of the trapezoid, which is 2 inches, or twice as long as the other sides. Except for the tan rhombus, which has two angles which that measure 150°, all of the shapes have angles whose measures are divisors of 360—120°, 90°, 60°, and 30°. Yet even these 150° angles relate to the other angles, since 150° is the sum of 90° and 60°.

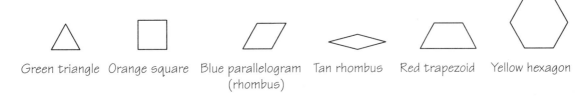

Green triangle | Orange square | Blue parallelogram (rhombus) | Tan rhombus | Red trapezoid | Yellow hexagon

These features of the Pattern Blocks encourage investigation of relationships among the shapes. One special aspect of the shapes is that the yellow block can be covered exactly by putting together two red blocks, or three blue blocks, or six green blocks. This is a natural lead-in to the consideration of how fractional parts relate to a whole—the yellow block. Thus, when children work only with the yellow, red, blue, and green blocks, and the yellow block is chosen as the unit, then a red block represents 1/2, a blue block represents 1/3, and a green block represents 1/6. Within this small world of fractions, children can develop hands-on familiarity and intuition about comparing fractions, finding equivalent fractions, changing improper fractions to mixed numbers, and modeling addition, subtraction, division, and multiplication of fractions.

Pattern Blocks provide a visual image which is essential for real understanding of fraction algorithms. Many children learn to do examples such as "3 1/2 = ?/2," "1/2 x 1/3 = ?" or "4 ÷ 1/3 = ?" at a purely symbolic level so that if they forget the procedure, they are at a total loss. Yet children who have had many presymbolic experiences solving problems such as "Find how many red blocks fit over three yellows and a red," "Find half of the blue block," or "Find how many blue blocks cover four yellow blocks" will have a solid intuitive foundation on which to build these skills and to fall back on if memory fails them.

1. How would you/could you sort the pattern blocks by angle?

By looking and consitrating on the blocks. By putting the blocks in patterns.

① You could sort the blocks by putting the acutes together, the obtuse angles together and the right angles together. It would be easier to figure out the questions.

From: Reach Into the Bag

Children do need ample time to experiment freely with Pattern Blocks, however, before they begin more serious investigations. Most children can begin without additional direction, but some may need suggestions. Asking children to find the different shapes, sizes, and colors of Pattern Blocks, or asking them to cover their desktops with the blocks or to find which blocks can be used to build straight roads, might be good for "starters."

WORKING WITH PATTERN BLOCKS

As children begin to work with Pattern Blocks, they use them primarily to explore spatial relations. Young children have an initial tendency to work with others and to copy one another's designs. Yet even duplicating another's pattern with blocks can expand a child's experience, develop ability to recognize similarities and differences, and provide a context for developing language related to geometric ideas. Throughout their investigations, children should be encouraged to talk about their constructions. Expressing their thoughts out loud helps children to clarify and extend their thinking.

Pattern Blocks help children to explore many mathematical topics, including congruence, similarity, symmetry, area, perimeter, patterns, functions, fractions, and graphing. The following are just a few of the possibilities:

When playing "exchange games" with the various sized blocks, children can develop an understanding of relationships between objects with different values, such as coins or place-value models.

When trying to identify which blocks can be put together to make another shape, children can begin to build a base for the concept of fractional pieces.

When the blocks are used to completely fill in an outline, the concept of area is developed. If children explore measuring the same area using different blocks as units they can develop understandings about the relationship of the size of the unit and the measure of the area.

When investigating the perimeter of shapes made with Pattern Blocks, children can discover that shapes with the same area can have different perimeters and that shapes with the same perimeter can have different areas.

When using Pattern Blocks to cover a flat surface, children can discover that some combinations of corners, or angles, fit together or can be arranged around a point. Knowing that a full circle measures 360° enables children to find the various angle measurements.

When finding how many blocks of the same color it takes to make a larger shape similar to the original block (which can be done with all but the yellow hexagon), children can discover the square number pattern—1, 4, 9, 16, ...

> When finding an equalateral shape I looked for equal sides. The word equalateral comes from the word equal meaning same or same size.

From: *Reach Into the Bag*

©1996 Cuisenaire Company of America, Inc.

ASSESSING CHILDREN'S UNDERSTANDING

The use of Pattern Blocks provides a perfect opportunity for authentic assessment. Watching children work with the blocks gives you a sense of how they approach a mathematical problem. Their thinking can be "seen" through their positioning of the Pattern Blocks. When a class breaks up into small working groups, you are able to circulate, listen, and raise questions, all the while focusing on how individuals are thinking.

The challenges that children encounter when working with Pattern Blocks often elicit unexpected abilities from children whose performance in more symbolic, number-oriented tasks may be weak. On the other hand, some children with good memories for numerical relationships have difficulty with spatial challenges and can more readily learn from freely exploring with Pattern Blocks. Thus, by observing children's free exploration, you can get a sense of individual styles and intellectual strengths.

Having children describe their creations and share their strategies and thinking with the whole class gives you another opportunity for observational assessment. Furthermore, you may want to gather children's recorded work or invite them to choose pieces to add to their math portfolios.

Square	Number of Blocks Added	Total Number of Blocks
1st	1	1
2nd	3	4
3rd	5	9
4th	7	16
5th	9	25
6th	11	36
7th	13	49
8th	15	64

From: *Square and Triangle Numbers*

You can multiply the number on the square collum by itself and you get the answer in the Total Number of Blocks collum.

If they dont it would become a rectangle.

100 because 10X10=100!

From: *Square and Triangle Numbers*

Models of teachers assessing children's understanding can be found in Cuisenaire's series of videotapes listed below.

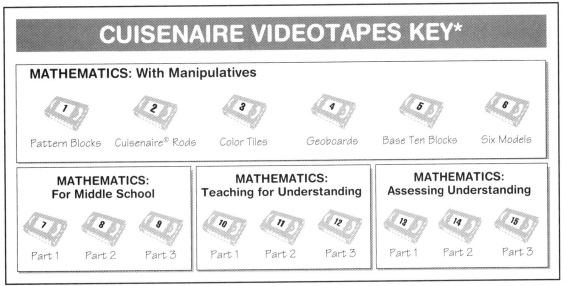

CUISENAIRE VIDEOTAPES KEY*

MATHEMATICS: With Manipulatives

| 1 Pattern Blocks | 2 Cuisenaire® Rods | 3 Color Tiles | 4 Geoboards | 5 Base Ten Blocks | 6 Six Models |

MATHEMATICS: For Middle School

| 7 Part 1 | 8 Part 2 | 9 Part 3 |

MATHEMATICS: Teaching for Understanding

| 10 Part 1 | 11 Part 2 | 12 Part 3 |

MATHEMATICS: Assessing Understanding

| 13 Part 1 | 14 Part 2 | 15 Part 3 |

*See *Overview of the Lessons*, pages 16–17, for specific lesson/video correlation.

STRANDS

Connect the Super Source™ to NCTM Standards.

	PROBLEM SOLVING	COMMUNICATION	REASONING	CONNECTIONS	Geometry	Logic	Measurement	Number	Patterns/Functions	Probability/Statistics
ALL POSSIBLE PERIMETERS	◆	◆	◆	◆	◆		◆			
ANGLES OF POLYGONS	◆	◆	◆	◆			◆		◆	
BUILDING HEXAGONS	◆	◆	◆	◆	◆					
BUILDING LARGER SHAPES	◆	◆	◆	◆					◆	
COMPARING AREAS	◆	◆	◆	◆	◆		◆	◆		
DON'T BREAK THE WAGON!	◆	◆	◆	◆		◆				
FILL THE HEXAGON	◆	◆	◆	◆	◆				◆	
FIND ALL THE PERIMETERS	◆	◆	◆	◆			◆			
FRACTION PUZZLES	◆	◆	◆	◆		◆		◆		
HOW MANY ANGLES?	◆	◆	◆	◆			◆	◆		
HOW MANY CAN SIT?	◆	◆	◆	◆	◆				◆	
LOOKING FOR SYMMETRY	◆	◆	◆	◆	◆					
PATTERN BLOCK ANGLES	◆	◆	◆	◆			◆			
PATTERN BLOCK RIDDLES	◆	◆	◆	◆	◆			◆	◆	
REACH INTO THE BAG	◆	◆	◆	◆			◆			
SQUARE AND TRIANGULAR NUMBERS	◆	◆	◆	◆	◆			◆	◆	
SURROUND	◆	◆	◆	◆	◆				◆	
WHAT'S MY VALUE?	◆	◆	◆	◆	◆		◆	◆		

TOPICS

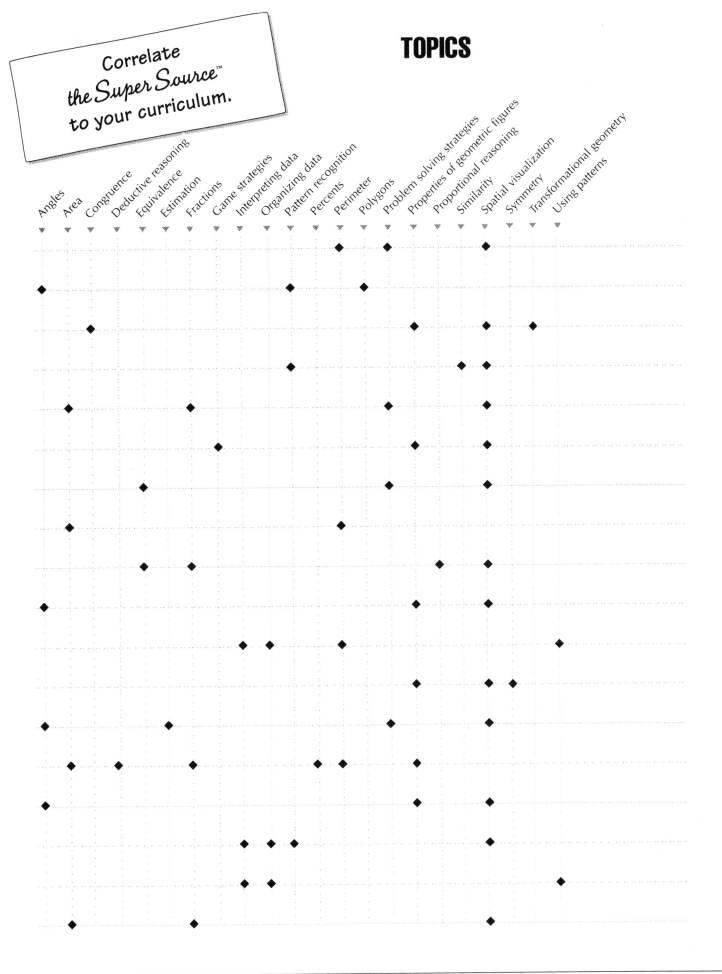

Classroom-tested activities contained in these *Super Source™* Pattern Blocks books focus on the math strands in the charts below.

…the Super Source™ **Pattern Blocks, Grades K-2**

Geometry	Logic	Measurement
Number	Patterns/Functions	Probability/Statistics

…the Super Source™ **Pattern Blocks, Grades 3-4**

Geometry	Logic	Measurement
Number	Patterns/Functions	Probability/Statistics

More SUPER SOURCE™ at a glance:
ADDITIONAL MANIPULATIVES for Grades 5-6

Classroom-tested activities contained in these *Super Source*™ books focus on the math strands as indicated in these charts.

the Super Source™ Snap™ Cubes, Grades 5-6

Geometry	Logic	Measurement
Number	Patterns/Functions	Probability/Statistics

the Super Source™ Cuisenaire® Rods, Grades 5-6

Geometry	Logic	Measurement
Number	Patterns/Functions	Probability/Statistics

the Super Source™ Geoboards, Grades 5-6

Geometry	Logic	Measurement
Number	Patterns/Functions	Probability/Statistics

the Super Source™ Color Tiles, Grades 5-6

Geometry	Logic	Measurement
Number	Patterns/Functions	Probability/Statistics

the Super Source™ Tangrams, Grades 5-6

Geometry	Logic	Measurement
Number	Patterns/Functions	Probability/Statistics

Overview of the Lessons

 See video key, page 11.

Pattern Blocks, Grades 5-6

See video key, page 11.

ALL POSSIBLE PERIMETERS

- • Perimeter
- • Spatial visualization
- • Problem solving strategies

Getting Ready

What You'll Need

Pattern Blocks, at least 6 of each shape per group

Pattern Block triangle paper, page 90

Crayons

Overhead Pattern Blocks (optional)

Overview

Children investigate the possible perimeters of shapes that can be made by using different combinations of the six Pattern Blocks. In this activity, children have the opportunity to:

- ◆ discover strategies for creating shapes having a range of perimeters
- ◆ generalize about characteristics of shapes having large and/or small perimeters

The Activity

You may want to have children work on this activity over the course of two or three sessions.

Introducing

- ◆ Review the concept of *perimeter* with the class.
- ◆ Review how the perimeter of Pattern Block shapes can be measured using the side of a green triangle as the unit of measurement.

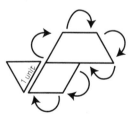

Perimeter = 7 units

On Their Own

> **What are all the possible perimeters of shapes that can be made using 6 Pattern Blocks?**
>
> - Working with your group, find all possible perimeters of shapes that can be made using 6 Pattern Blocks. You may use as many different combinations of blocks as you like.
>
> - Be sure to fit your blocks together so that each block shares at least 1 full unit of length with another block.
>
> - Copy the shapes you make onto triangle paper and color them in. Figure out and record the perimeter of each shape.
>
> - Be ready to discuss strategies you used for making shapes with new perimeters.

The Bigger Picture

Thinking and Sharing

Ask children to tell what perimeters they found. List these perimeters on the chalkboard in numerical order. Allow groups to compare some of the shapes they made, especially those that produced perimeters not found by other groups.

Use prompts such as these to promote class discussion:

- What was the smallest perimeter you found, and how did you make the shape that had this perimeter? Is it possible to get this perimeter in any other way? Why or why not?

- What was the largest perimeter you found, and how did you make the shape that had this perimeter? Is it possible to get this perimeter in any other way? Why or why not?

- What other perimeters did you find?

- What strategies, if any, did you use to find new perimeters?

- What discoveries did you make?

- How do you know that you have found all possible perimeters?

Writing

Ask children to write about a discovery that they made in the course of this activity.

Point out that each of the three sets is the same, except that a different 4-sided block is used in each set. Ask children to consider this when predicting how the lists of possible perimeters may compare.

Extending the Activity

1. Have children work in groups to predict, explore, and then compare, the possible perimeters of shapes made with each of the following sets of blocks:

> (a) two hexagons, one trapezoid, one triangle, one tan rhombus
> (b) two hexagons, one trapezoid, one triangle, one blue rhombus
> (c) two hexagons, one trapezoid, one triangle, one square

Where's the Mathematics?

Children may realize that the smallest possible perimeter will be the perimeter of a shape made with six triangles, as triangles are the blocks with the least number of sides. They may discover that although the triangles can be arranged in different ways, only one way will produce the smallest perimeter, that being 6 units.

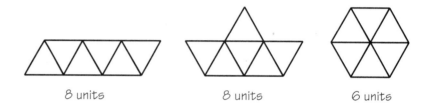

| 8 units | 8 units | 6 units |

Children may also predict and discover that the greatest possible perimeter will be the perimeter of a shape made with six hexagons, as hexagons have the greatest number of sides. Although the hexagons can be arranged in different ways, only one arrangement will yield the maximum possible perimeter of 26 units.

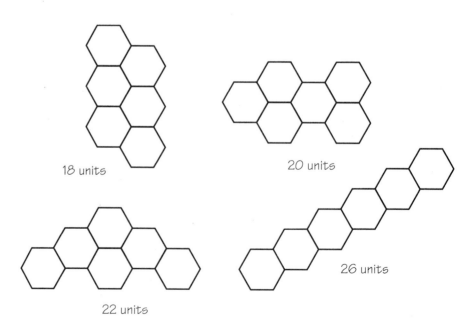

18 units

20 units

22 units

26 units

©1996 Cuisenaire Company of America, Inc.

2. Challenge children to find the minimum and maximum perimeters of shapes that can made using one of each of the six different Pattern Blocks.

Some children may use trial and error to build shapes that have different perimeters. They may select different assortments of blocks, and use them to build a variety of shapes, calculating and recording the perimeters as they work. Other children may develop a more systematic way of searching for the possible perimeters. For example, if children have discovered that six triangles can be arranged to form a shape with a perimeter of 8 units, they may realize that they can exchange one of their triangles for a four-sided block, producing a new shape with a perimeter that is 1 unit larger. They could continue this kind of exchanging until they have a shape made of six 4-sided blocks and then start exchanging these for other shapes.

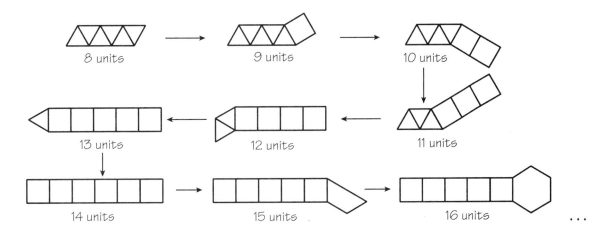

As children experiment with different ways of arranging the blocks, they may discover that shapes that are more compact will have smaller perimeters than those that are more elongated. Children may use this observation to build and alter their shapes to produce new shapes with larger or smaller perimeters. Although there is only one way to make a shape that has the smallest perimeter (6 units), and one way to make the shape with the largest perimeter (26 units), there are multiple ways of arranging the blocks to form shapes that have some of the other perimeters. Children should find that perimeters that lie towards the middle of the range of possible perimeters can be obtained by arranging the shapes in the widest variety of different ways.

ANGLES OF POLYGONS

- Angles
- Polygons
- Pattern recognition

Getting Ready

What You'll Need

Pattern Blocks, several of each shape per child

Overhead Pattern Blocks (optional)

Overview

Children investigate the sums of the measure of the interior angles in a variety of polygons. In this activity, children have the opportunity to:

- ◆ build polygons containing angles of various sizes
- ◆ develop strategies for measuring angles
- ◆ find patterns and use them to make predictions

The Activity

Before doing this activity, children should have successfully completed Pattern Block Angles, page 66 or should have a good understanding of angle measurement. It would be helpful for children to have worked on How Many Angles?, page 54 as well.

To copy their polygons, suggest that children trace around the shape on a piece of paper, or make a dot at each vertex and then connect the dots using a straight edge.

Introducing

- ◆ Review what children have learned about the angles of the various Pattern Block shapes.

- ◆ Ask different groups of children to find the sums of the measures of the angles of one of the following Pattern Blocks: the triangle, the square, or the blue parallelogram. Record this information in a table on the chalkboard, as shown.

shape	name of polygon	# of sides	sum of angle measures
△	triangle	3	180°
□	square	4	360°
▱	parallelogram	4	360°

- ◆ Now display a polygon made with a square and a blue parallelogram. Have children make the same design with their Pattern Blocks and copy it onto a piece of paper.

- ◆ Ask children to figure out the sum of the measures of the angles of their six-sided polygon.

- ◆ Invite volunteers to share their results.

On Their Own

> **What can you discover about the sum of the measures of the angles of polygons made from Pattern Blocks?**
>
> - Working with a partner, find the sum of the measures of the angles of each of the Pattern Block shapes. Record your findings.
>
> - Next, combine different numbers of Pattern Blocks in various ways to make other polygons.
>
> - Copy each of your polygons onto paper and work with your partner to figure out the measures of each of the angles. Record these measures on your drawings.
>
> - Now figure out and record the sum of the measures of the angles for each polygon. Also record the number of sides each polygon has.
>
> - Look for patterns as you work.

The Bigger Picture

Thinking and Sharing

Ask one pair to pick one of their shapes and tell how many sides it has and what the sum of its angle measures is. Record this information on the chalkboard. Ask other pairs, one by one, to tell about one of their shapes. Continue to list the results until all the pairs have told about the shapes they made. Then ask children to help you organize the results into a table, listing their polygons in order from those having the fewest number of sides to those having the greatest, and recording the sum of the angle measures of each polygon. Allow children time to examine the table, discuss the results, and share observations.

Use prompts such as these to promote class discussion:

- How did you go about finding the measures of the angles in your polygons?

- Were some angle measures easier/harder to determine than others? Which ones? Why?

- Do all the numbers on the table seem to fit? Why or why not?

- What do you notice about the results? What patterns do you see?

- Based on the class results, what generalizations might you make?

Writing

Have children explain how they might use their results to figure out the sum of the measures of the angles of a polygon with 20 sides without using the Pattern Blocks.

Extending the Activity

1. Have groups build polygons using one of each of the six different Pattern Block shapes and figure out the sums of the measures of the angles in each polygon. Ask children to decide whether their polygons fit the pattern produced by the other polygons in the table.

Where's the Mathematics?

As children work with the Pattern Blocks to build polygons that have different-sized angles, they may notice the difference between angles of convex polygons and angles of concave polygons.

Convex polygons   Concave polygons

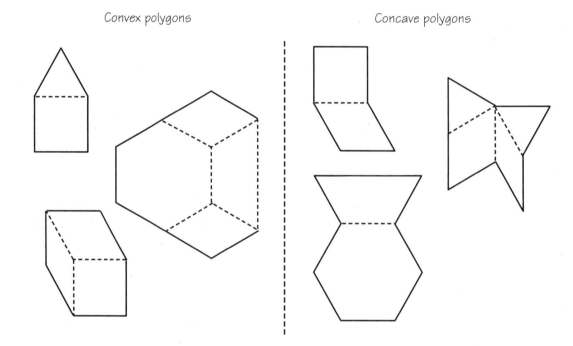

In a convex polygon, all of the interior angles have measures less than 180°, whereas in a concave polygon, one or more angles measures more than 180°. It is these larger angles that children may have difficulty measuring. If they see them as simply combinations of the angles of the blocks from which they were made, children may just add up these smaller measures. Some children may instead figure out the measure of obtuse angles based on how much bigger they are than 180°. To do this, they may use the long side of the trapezoid or a straight edge to extend one side of the angle, and use one of the other Pattern Blocks to measure the remaining part of the angle.

2. Have children build as many different six-sided polygons as they can and use them to prove or disprove the theory that the sum of the measures of the interior angles of any hexagon will always be 720°.

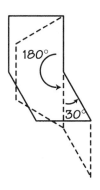

As the groups compile their results, children should notice that for polygons having the same number of sides, the sum of the measures of the angles is the same. This may lead them to question results that do not seem to fit this rule. Some children may also notice that the sums are multiples of 180° and that there is an increase of 180° in the sum each time a side is added. Identification of this pattern will allow children to check their individual results and to extend the class chart for polygons of other sizes.

Number of sides in polygon	Sum of angle measures
3	180
4	360
5	540
6	720
7	900
8	1080
9	1260
10	1440

The sum of the measures of the interior angles of any polygon can be found by subtracting 2 from the number of sides of the polygon, and multiplying that difference by 180°. Although children should not be expected to discover this formula, some children may find it interesting and may wish to verify it using their results.

BUILDING HEXAGONS

- Properties of geometric figures
- Spatial visualization
- Congruence
- Transformational geometry

Getting Ready

What You'll Need

Pattern Blocks, at least 3 of each shape per pair

Overhead Pattern Blocks (optional)

Overview

Children investigate ways of making hexagons using different numbers of blocks. In this activity, children have the opportunity to:

- explore how smaller polygons fit together to make larger polygons

- learn about transformations and congruence by investigating to see whether shapes are flips or turns of each other

The Activity

You may want to have one child show his or her hexagon on the overhead using transparent blocks. Invite children who think they have different solutions to display them, as well. Volunteers might then be asked to demonstrate how a flip and/or turn will show that the hexagons are congruent.

Introducing

- Show children the yellow Pattern Block, and elicit that it is a hexagon. Explain that it is a *regular* hexagon because it has six equal sides and six equal angles.

- Point out that any polygon with six sides is a hexagon, even though it may look very different from the yellow block.

- Ask children to use a square and a blue parallelogram to make a hexagon.

- Have children compare their shapes. Establish that there's only one way to build a hexagon using these two blocks. Show how any of the arrangements can be turned and/or flipped so that it will fit exactly on top of another. Tell children that shapes that match like this are said to be *congruent*.

On Their Own

> ### How many ways can you think of to build hexagons using your Pattern Blocks?
>
> - Working with your partner, build hexagons in as many different ways as you can first with 1 block, then 2 blocks, and then 3 blocks.
>
> - Be sure to join blocks so that each block shares an entire unit of length with another. (Remember that the trapezoid has 2 units of length on its long side.)
>
> - Trace around the blocks to record your solutions on paper. Check to make sure none of your solutions are congruent.
>
> - Be prepared to talk about how you know that you've found all possible solutions.

The Bigger Picture

Thinking and Sharing

Ask children to tell how they "built" a hexagon using only one block (the only solution being to use the yellow hexagon.) Then have children take turns sharing their hexagons made with two blocks and then those made with three blocks. Children can post the solutions they traced, or rebuild them with transparent blocks on the overhead.

Use prompts such as these to promote class discussion:

- What solutions did you find for two blocks? for three blocks?

- How did you go about finding solutions? Did you organize your search in some particular way? If so, tell about it.

- How did you check to make sure none of your solutions were congruent?

- Do you think you found all the possible solutions? Why or why not?

- Is there a limit to the number of blocks you could use to build a hexagon? Explain your answer.

- What other discoveries did you make?

Writing

Ask children to describe three things they discovered about making hexagons with Pattern Blocks.

Extending the Activity

1. Challenge children to build other polygons—pentagons, heptagons, and so on—using different numbers of Pattern Blocks. Have them record their polygons and post the different solutions they find.

Where's the Mathematics?

Although the only way to make a hexagon with one block is to use the yellow block, there are many ways to make hexagons using two or three blocks. Children may not find them all, or may not realize that they have found them all. However, there may be some children who work systematically, and may therefore feel certain that they have found all possible solutions. For example, a child may make a hexagon using a square and a blue parallelogram, and then try combining the square with every other block to find all possible 2-block hexagons that can be made using a square. He or she then might try putting the blue parallelogram together with each of the remaining blocks to see if any of these combinations make hexagons. The child may then go on to test other combinations using other blocks in the same way.

Children may realize that some of their 2-block hexagons can be extended using a second block of one of the shapes in the original arrangement. For example, the 2-block hexagon shown below can be extended to a 3-block hexagon by adding either another square or another parallelogram as shown. Some children may notice that no matter how many squares or parallelograms are added in this way, the shape will still be a hexagon.

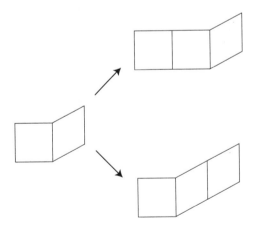

As children work with the blocks, they may begin to see relationships between their attributes and be able to predict—even before putting certain blocks together—whether the blocks will fit together to make a shape with six sides. For example, after discovering that three squares can be used to make a hexagon, children may hypothesize that three blocks of any one of the four-sided shapes can also be fitted together to make a hexagon. This proves to be the case.

2. Ask children to make the smallest hexagon they can using eight Pattern Blocks. Then ask them to make the largest hexagon they can using eight Pattern Blocks. Ask them to find the difference between the areas of the two hexagons, given that the triangle has an area of 1 square unit.

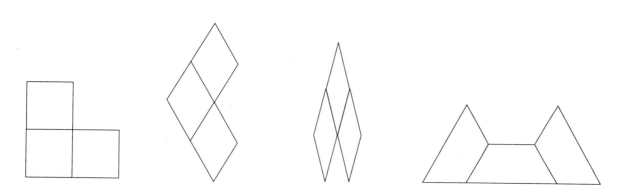

Children may then move on to investigate 3-block shapes formed by combining different four-sided blocks. Here they may find that similar arrangements of different combinations of shapes do not always produce hexagons. Other arrangements need to be explored. For instance, a trapezoid placed above two squares makes a hexagon; but a trapezoid placed above two parallelograms does not.

The parallelograms slant in such a way that one of the sides of one of the parallelograms continues a side of the trapezoid. However, the trapezoid can be used with parallelograms to form a hexagon, by arranging the blocks in a different way, as shown below.

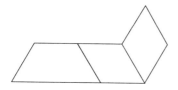

To check for congruence, children may compare newly-made shapes to those already recorded. Whereas some children may be able to recognize congruence just by inspection, others may need to test by flipping and/or rotating their shapes to see if they match exactly. This experience will help children in their future work with transformational geometry.

BUILDING LARGER SHAPES

Getting Ready

What You'll Need

Pattern Blocks, 1 set per group
Overhead Pattern Blocks (optional)

Overview

Children investigate the number of blocks needed to build shapes that are similar to each of the individual Pattern Block shapes. In this activity, children have the opportunity to:

◆ investigate the idea of similarity

◆ develop strategies to prove that two shapes are similar

◆ discover and use patterns to make predictions and solve problems

The Activity

Children can also check for similarity by measuring the sides of the original blocks and comparing them to those of the enlargements. If all of the sides have been enlarged by the same factor, (for example, if one side has been doubled the other sides have also been doubled), then the shapes are similar.

Introducing

◆ Ask children to use the square Pattern Blocks to make several squares of different sizes.

◆ Discuss the squares children have made, and record the numbers of blocks needed for each.

◆ Explain that all squares are *similar*, because, regardless of their size, they have *exactly* the same shape.

◆ Show children that their enlargements are all similar to the square Pattern Block by having them try the sighting method to check for similarity: have children hold a single square above a larger square, close one eye, and move the single square toward or away fro the larger square until the larger square seems to be exactly covered by the single square. If the two can be made to appear the same size, they are similar.

On Their Own

Can you build enlargements of each of the Pattern Block shapes?

- Work with a group. Try to build 4 different enlargements of each shape in your Pattern Block set. Use only blocks of the original shape in your enlargements.

- Remember that the new, larger shapes must be similar to the original blocks, and therefore must have exactly the same shape as the original block.

- Record your enlargements by tracing them onto white paper. Record the number of blocks you use for each enlargement.

- Look for patterns as you work.

The Bigger Picture

Thinking and Sharing

Discuss which shapes can and cannot be enlarged. Have children compare the number of blocks used for each enlargement and discuss any patterns they noticed that may have helped them in making larger shapes.

Use prompts such as these to promote class discussion:

- For which blocks were you able to make larger shapes that were similar to the original block?

- Which block could not be used to make larger, similar shapes? Why do you think it's impossible to make enlargements of this shape?

- How did you decide whether each shape you made was similar to the original block?

- What pattern, if any, did you notice in the numbers of blocks used to build increasingly larger shapes?

- How did this pattern help you to build other shapes?

Writing

Ask children to explain how they could use the pattern they discovered to determine the number of blocks it would take to make the tenth larger similar shape, if a single block is considered to be the first shape.

Extending the Activity

1. Suggest that children attempt to build enlargements of the yellow hexagon using a mixture of Pattern Blocks.

Where's the Mathematics?

Children are likely to go through a considerable process of trial and error as they work. Through their investigation, they discover that it is possible to build enlargements of all the blocks except the hexagon. Some children may come to notice a pattern in the number of blocks needed to build each similar shape (the square numbers—1, 4, 9, 16, 25, and so on) and use this knowledge to figure out how many blocks should be in each future enlargement.

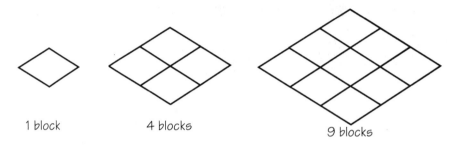

1 block   4 blocks   9 blocks

This may make the task of building similar shapes easier, but will not eliminate trial and error.

Some children may devise the following rule for finding the number of blocks needed to make their enlargements: The number of blocks in any given enlargement can be determined by squaring the number of that enlargement in the series. For example, if the enlargement is the tenth possible similar shape, the number of blocks needed to build it is 10 x 10, or 100. The numbers grow as they do because in each enlargement, one more row of blocks is being added in each direction.

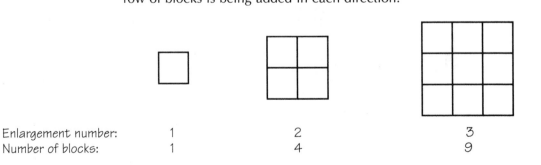

| Enlargement number: | 1 | 2 | 3 | ... |
| Number of blocks: | 1 | 4 | 9 | ... |

2. Challenge children to build similar hexagons, each made from only one kind of Pattern Block. Encourage children to look for and share any relationships they might see between the number of blocks they used, and the number of blocks used in enlargements of other shapes.

Children may have difficulty building enlargements of the trapezoid block. They may well make several larger trapezoids that are not similar to the single trapezoid because their sides have not increased proportionally. For example, in the trapezoid shown on the right below, the left and right sides are three times as long as the corresponding sides of the trapezoid block, the top side is four times as long as the top side of the trapezoid block, and the bottom side is three and one-half times as long as the bottom side of the trapezoid block.

You may want to explain to children that two polygons are similar if their corresponding angles are congruent and their corresponding sides are proportional.

 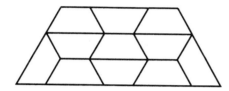

Children will need to realize that since one side of the trapezoid block is twice as long as each of the other three, this must also be the case in any similar trapezoids. The trapezoids shown below are all similar to the Pattern Block trapezoid.

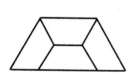

4 blocks

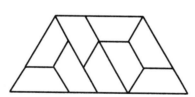

9 blocks

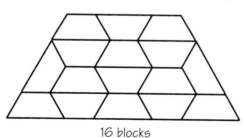

16 blocks

COMPARING AREAS

- Fractions
- Area
- Problem solving strategies
- Spatial visualization

Getting Ready

What You'll Need

Pattern Blocks, several of each shape per pair

Overhead Pattern Blocks (optional)

Overview

Children investigate the relationship between the areas of two pairs of two different Pattern Blocks. In this activity, children have the opportunity to:

- ◆ devise strategies for comparing areas
- ◆ determine fractional parts of areas

The Activity

Introducing

- ◆ Review the concept of area with children. Establish that the area of a shape is the amount of surface that it covers.
- ◆ Ask children to tell which two Pattern Blocks have the greatest area. Have them explain how they know this.

On Their Own

> **Can you solve these challenging area problems?**
>
> - Working with a partner, use your Pattern Blocks to answer the following questions:
>
>   **Question 1:** Which has a greater area, a blue parallelogram or a square?
>
>   **Question 2:** What fractional part of the area of the square is the area of the tan rhombus?
>
> - Find a way to justify your answers.
>
> - Be ready to explain your conclusions.

The Bigger Picture

Thinking and Sharing

Call on a pair of partners to answer the first question and to show how they can justify their answer. If other members of the class have different answers or different ways of proving their answer, invite them to share their work, as well. Repeat this process with the second question.

Use prompts such as these to promote class discussion:

- Which has the greater area, the blue parallelogram or the square? How can you prove your answer is correct?

- Can you tell just by looking at the square and the tan rhombus what fractional part the rhombus is of the square? Explain your answer.

- How did you determine what fraction of the area of the square the area of the tan rhombus is? How can you prove your answer is correct?

- Did you find either of your results surprising? If so, why?

- What do the three shapes you worked with have in common? What does your investigation tell you about the area of shapes that are alike in this way?

Extending the Activity

1. Have children put the six different Pattern Blocks in order from least area to greatest area and explain why they arranged them as they did.

2. Have children select a block to use as a unit measure of area, and build designs having different areas, using as many different Pattern Blocks as they can in their designs.

Where's the Mathematics?

The questions posed in this activity provide children with an opportunity to devise and conduct their own exploration into what at first may appear to be two simple comparisons. It is likely that children will be unable to answer either question merely by looking at the blocks. Furthermore, they may find that they need to use other Pattern Blocks to help them find the answers. Most importantly, children will need to develop some strategies for comparing areas.

To answer the first question, children may lay the blue parallelogram on top of the square, aligning the shorter diagonal of the parallelogram with a side of the square (as shown below) in an effort to determine the relationship between the square and half of the parallelogram.

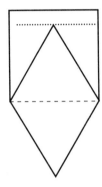

Children will see that the point of the parallelogram doesn't reach the edge of the square. The bottom half of the parallelogram, if divided into halves, could fill in the right-triangular regions that are not covered, but the rectangle formed by the pieces of the parallelogram would not reach the top of the square. Children could therefore conclude that the square has a greater area than the blue parallelogram.

Another way children might try to prove the square is larger than the parallelogram is by using three triangles and a square. The square can be laid on top of a row of three triangles joined to form a trapezoid, with one edge of the square aligned with the shorter base of the trapezoid (see picture below). The square will cover the middle triangle and half of each of the other two triangles. That total area is the same as the area of a blue parallelogram. However, the square will extend past the height of the triangles, proving that it is larger than the parallelogram.

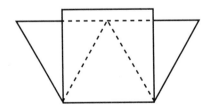

One way children might show that the area of the tan rhombus is one-half the area of the orange square, is to build the following two figures:

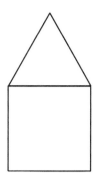 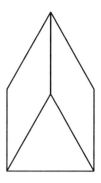

These two figures are congruent. Children can build one on top of the other and see that they match exactly. If they remove the green triangle from each of the figures, they will be left with one orange square and two tan rhombuses. As these remaining shapes must be equal in area, one tan rhombus must be equal in area to one-half of a square.

It is possible that some children might use formulas for area to prove that the area of the tan rhombus is one-half the area of the square. If they use the length of a side of the square as their unit of measure, children can determine that the square has an area of 1 square unit. Comparing the dimensions of the tan rhombus to those of the square, children may see that the base of the rhombus is equal in length to the side of the square (1 unit long), and, since two rhombuses placed one above the other are equal in height to the square, the height of one rhombus is 1/2 of a unit. Multiplying the base by the height, children will find the area of the tan rhombus to be 1/2 square unit.

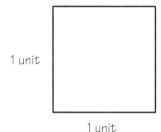

1 unit

1 unit

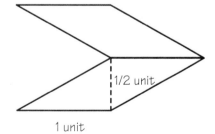

1/2 unit

1 unit

Children might also answer both questions by tracing around the Pattern Blocks on paper and cutting or folding the paper shapes to compare areas. They may try to fill the outline of one of the shapes with pieces of the other. In using this strategy, children focus on the idea of area as the amount of space inside a shape. Children may be surprised to discover the differences in the areas of the three quadrilaterals, especially if they realize that all three are rhombuses with the same perimeter.

DON'T BREAK THE WAGON!

- Game strategies
- Properties of geometric figures
- Spatial visualization

Getting Ready

What You'll Need

Pattern Blocks, at least 3 hexagons, 8 blue parallelograms, 6 trapezoids, and 10 triangles per pair

Don't Break the Wagon! game board, page 92

Overhead Pattern Blocks/Overhead transparency of *Don't Break the Wagon!* game board (optional)

Overview

Children play a game in which they use Pattern Blocks to cover a game board, and develop strategies that will enable them to avoid having to take the last turn. In this activity, children have the opportunity to:

- ◆ use spatial reasoning
- ◆ find combinations of shapes that will cover a region
- ◆ develop strategic thinking skills

The Activity

Introducing

- ◆ Show children a *Don't Break the Wagon!* game board. Model how the pieces can be placed on the board by putting one trapezoid on one of the "wagon wheels."

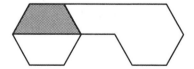

- ◆ Have children work together to find different ways of filling up the game board.
- ◆ Ask several volunteers to show their work.

On Their Own

Play *Don't Break the Wagon!*

Here are the rules.

1. This is a game for 2 players. The object of the game is to try to *not* be the player who goes last.

2. Players decide who will go first.

3. Players take turns placing blocks on the game board. The blocks must fit within the outline, with at least one edge of each block touching the outline.

4. The player who places the last block on the board "breaks the wagon" and loses.

- Play the game at least 5 times. Take turns going first. For each game, record who went first, and whether that player won or lost.

- Try playing 5 more games with a different partner. For each game, record who went first, and whether that player won or lost.

- Be ready to talk about good moves, bad moves, and winning strategies.

The Bigger Picture

Thinking and Sharing

Invite children to talk about their games and describe some of the thinking they did.

Use prompts such as these to promote class discussion:

- How did you decide which blocks to play first?
- Did your strategy change as the board became more full? If so, how?
- As you got closer to the end of the game, could you predict who would win? How?
- Is it better to go first or second? Why do you think that?
- What strategies did you use to help you win?

Writing

Have children write about a strategy they used in one of their games and describe how well it did or did not pan out.

Extending the Activity

1. Have children play a variation of the game in which the person who places the last block wins. Ask children how this change affected their strategies for winning.

Teacher Talk

Where's the Mathematics?

This game helps children develop strategies involving spatial reasoning. Many children will begin without a given strategy; as they play they will have an opportunity to test different strategies. For example, children may at first lose because they fill the game board with "obvious fits"—larger shapes—without recognizing that there may be other ways to fill the spaces.

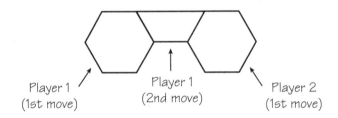

Player 1 loses because he or she has played the final block.

However, children may soon recognize that using a smaller shape to fill part of the remaining space can force the other player to play the last piece.

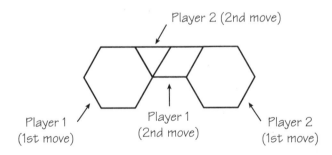

Player 2 loses because he or she has played the final block.

2. Have children create and use their own game boards.

Children may develop and test many different strategies. For example, in an extension of the strategy shown above, children may attempt to place blocks in a way that leaves "holes" that their partner has to fill. In the game shown below, Player 1 has just played the green triangle marked with an asterisk (*). This play forces Player 2 to fill one of the open spaces with a triangle. Player 1 can then play another triangle, leaving the last open space for Player 2.

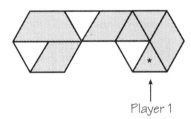

Player 1

Player 2 will be forced to play the final block.

Some children may feel that they have more control over the outcome of the game if they continually play smaller blocks. While this may allow for a wider choice of moves on each turn, children soon learn that it is more often the placement of the piece (not necessarily its size) that makes for a good move. Depending on the play of the game, good moves can be made with both large and small blocks.

After playing several games, some children may recognize the advantage in going second. The player who goes second has an opportunity to react to each play made by his or her opponent. This can prove valuable when the player who goes second is playing with a particular strategy in mind. By going second, he or she can force the game to play out favorably.

FILL THE HEXAGON

- Equivalence
- Spatial visualization
- Problem solving strategies

Getting Ready

What You'll Need

Pattern Blocks (no orange or tan), about 100 per group

Hexagon outline, page 93

Overhead Pattern Blocks (optional)

Overview

Children investigate ways of filling a hexagon-shaped outline with Pattern Blocks. In this activity, children have the opportunity to:

- experiment with equivalence
- recognize and use patterns to solve problems
- discover that patterns generated within the context of a problem may produce numbers that are not viable solutions

The Activity

Introducing

- Give children copies of the hexagon outline and ask them to speculate about how they could fill it with the fewest possible Pattern Blocks.
- Then challenge children to predict the largest number of blocks that could fill the outline, and to give reasons for their thinking.

On Their Own

> How many different numbers of Pattern Blocks can you use to fill the hexagon outline?
>
> - Working with a small group, try to fill the hexagon outline with every possible number of blocks, from the fewest to the greatest. You can use any combination of yellow, red, blue, and green blocks.
>
> - Record both the kinds of blocks and the number of blocks you use each time you fill the hexagon.
>
> - Watch for patterns and other ways to make your task easier.

The Bigger Picture

Thinking and Sharing

Have groups take turns sharing their solutions for various numbers of blocks used to fill the hexagon outline. List these solutions on the chalkboard. Invite children to describe the strategies they used in approaching the problem.

Use prompts such as these to promote class discussion:

- What systems, if any, did you have for finding solutions?

- Do you think you have found all the ways of filling the hexagon? Why or why not?

- What number of blocks do you think would provide the most solutions?

- What discoveries did you make as you searched for solutions? What patterns did you notice?

Extending the Activity

1. Have small groups each choose three or four numbers and try to find all the different ways the hexagon outline can be filled using exactly those numbers of blocks. Groups could then share their data and collectively find all the possible ways of filling the outline.

2. Have children build a hexagon with sides three times as long as a side of the green triangle using only hexagons and blue parallelograms. Challenge children to determine the least and the greatest number of blocks needed to do this.

3. Suggest children make a graph showing the possible solutions to the problem in the activity for each number of blocks between 6 and 24. Each solution should be colored on triangle paper, and posted on the graph. Children can continue to find solutions and add them to the graph over a period of time.

Where's the Mathematics?

Although there is only one way to fill the hexagon outline with 6 blocks and only one way with 24 blocks, there are many ways to fill it with some of the other numbers of blocks between 6 and 24. However, no one group of children should be expected to find all possible solutions. As they work at solving the problem and share their findings with other groups, children will realize that there are multiple ways to fill the hexagon. The solutions listed on the chalkboard should point to the fact that numbers in the middle of the range have more solutions than numbers closer to 6 or to 24.

As children work on the problem, they may come to see that they can use equivalences among the blocks to develop systematic ways of finding new solutions. For example, children may realize that if 24 triangles will fill the hexagon and if one blue parallelogram is equivalent in area to two triangles, then 1 blue parallelogram and 22 triangles will also fill the hexagon.

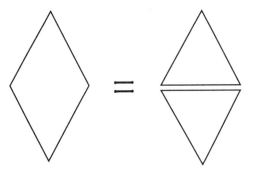

By substituting a second blue parallelogram for two more triangles, a new solution—2 blue parallelograms and 20 triangles—can be found. Successive substitutions will result in 3 blue parallelograms and 18 triangles, then 4 blue parallelograms and 16 triangles, and so on. As they continue to make these substitutions, many children will likely see a pattern in the numbers: A solution for each consecutively smaller number of blocks can be found by adding one blue parallelogram and subtracting two triangles. These children may then decide to use this pattern to generate the remaining solutions in the sequence without using the blocks.

If children model the patterns with the blocks, they will find that not all numerical combinations translate into actual solutions. For example, although it is possible for children to fill the hexagon with 1 hexagon and 18 triangles, with 2 hexagons and 12 triangles, and with 3 hexagons and 6 triangles, children will not be able to fill the outline with 4 hexagons and 0 triangles, as the pattern might suggest.

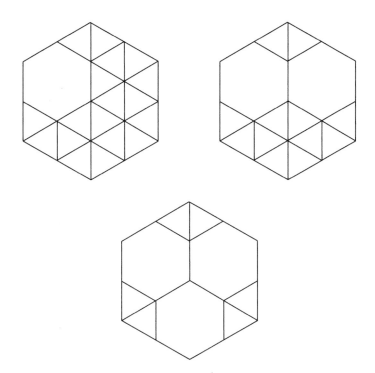

Children who work systematically will not all have the same system. Some children might ignore the patterns and first use just one kind of block, then all combinations of two kinds of blocks, then all combinations of three kinds of blocks, and so on. Other children may begin by filling in the outline with the biggest blocks they can, and then replacing them, one by one, with successively smaller blocks which, when put together, form the same shape. However children work, many of them will agree that having a system makes the problem easier to solve.

FIND ALL THE PERIMETERS

Getting Ready

What You'll Need

Pattern Blocks (no orange or tan), about 20 per pair

Pattern Block triangle paper, page 90

Crayons

Scissors

Overhead Pattern Blocks (optional)

Overview

Children use specific Pattern Blocks to create shapes with as many different perimeters as possible. In this activity, children have the opportunity to:

- explore the relationship between the compactness of a shape and its perimeter

- use non-standard units of measure to find perimeter

- discover that shapes that have the same area can have different perimeters

The Activity

Introducing

- Make a shape using 1 red trapezoid, 1 blue parallelogram, and 1 green triangle. Make sure that each block shares at least one full unit of length with another block.

- Demonstrate how to find the perimeter of a shape using the edge of a green triangle as a unit of measure, as shown.

- Ask children to find the perimeter of their shapes.

On Their Own

What happens to the perimeter when you arrange the same set of blocks to make different shapes?

- With a partner, find all the different shapes you can make using 1 yellow hexagon, 2 red trapezoids, 3 blue parallelograms, and 4 green triangles.

- In each shape, make sure that each block shares at least 1 full unit of length with another block.

Okay   Okay   Not okay

- Find the perimeter of each of your shapes using the edge of a green triangle as the unit of measure.

- Each time you find a shape with a different perimeter, record it by coloring it on triangle paper.

- Cut out your shapes and label their perimeters.

The Bigger Picture

Thinking and Sharing

Ask children to tell the smallest perimeter they found. Begin a class chart by writing the smallest perimeter mentioned on the far left, and inviting children who have shapes with this perimeter to post them under this heading. Ask for the next smallest perimeter found, label a new column, and have children post any shapes that have this perimeter. Continue the chart until shapes with all the different perimeters children found have been posted.

Use prompts such as these to promote class discussion:

- What do you notice when you look at the posted shapes?

- How can you describe the shapes with the least perimeter and the shapes with the greatest perimeter?

- Did you have a strategy for finding different perimeters? If so, describe it.

- What do you notice about the areas of all the shapes?

Writing

Ask children to describe how they would arrange a set of Pattern Blocks to produce a shape that has a small perimeter and a shape that has a large perimeter.

Extending the Activity

Have children explore the perimeters of shapes that can be made using 12 orange squares.

Teacher Talk

Where's the Mathematics?

There are many different shapes that can be made with the ten Pattern Blocks. The possible perimeters of these shapes range from 12 units to 22 units. Here is an example of a shape with the least perimeter and a shape with the greatest perimeter:

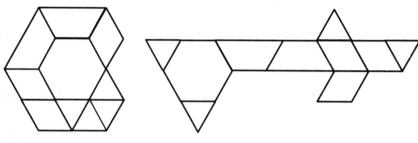

Perimeter = 12 units   Perimeter = 22 units

Although children may begin their search by randomly building different shapes and finding their perimeters, they may at some point try to produce new perimeters by making changes to existing shapes. For example, if a child has made shape A below, he or she may move one of the red trapezoids, creating shape B, and, in doing so, produce a shape with a perimeter that is 2 units larger. From there, shape C can be created by moving one of the green triangles, producing a shape with a perimeter that is 2 units larger than that of shape B.

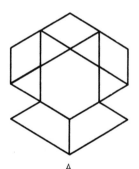

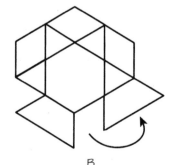

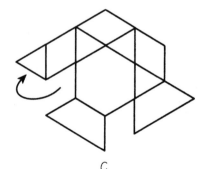

A
Perimeter = 14 units

B
Perimeter = 16 units

C
Perimeter = 18 units

As they rearrange the blocks, children see how the perimeter is affected by sides that become exposed or concealed by the change in the arrangement. This may lead them to discover that when the blocks are arranged so that many of their sides are concealed, the shape will have a smaller perimeter than if many sides of the blocks are exposed. It may also help them to figure out ways to rearrange blocks in existing arrangements to produce a shape with either a larger or smaller perimeter. For example, if the parallelogram on the end of shape D below is relocated as shown in E, it will have only two exposed sides as compared to three in shape D. In addition, it will conceal two sides instead of one, resulting in a net reduction of 2 units of perimeter.

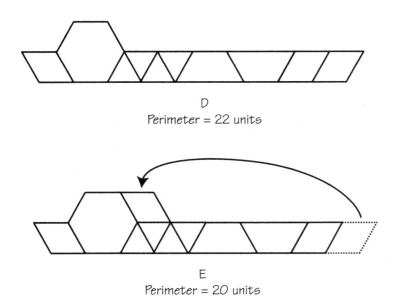

D
Perimeter = 22 units

E
Perimeter = 20 units

In examining the class chart, children may notice that the shapes with the smaller perimeters are more compact than the shapes with greater perimeters. Furthermore, they may see that as the shapes get longer and longer, their perimeters get larger and larger. Children may be able to reason that the compact shapes have smaller perimeters because each block in the arrangement is surrounded by several other blocks, therefore there are fewer exposed sides to be counted in the perimeter. In elongated shapes, most of the blocks have more than one exposed side, making for greater perimeter.

FRACTION PUZZLES

- Fractions
- Equivalence
- Proportional reasoning
- Spatial visualization

Getting Ready

What You'll Need

Pattern Blocks, about 12 green, blue, and red blocks per pair

Pattern Block triangle paper, page 90

Crayons

Scissors

Overhead Pattern Blocks (optional)

Overview

Children solve Pattern Block puzzles that require them to build shapes in which certain blocks comprise specific fractional parts of the whole shape. In this activity, children have the opportunity to:

- ◆ discover fractional equivalents
- ◆ explore relationships among the areas of different shapes
- ◆ use ratios and proportions to solve problems

The Activity

Introducing

- ◆ Build this Pattern Block shape using four green triangles.
- ◆ Ask children what fractional part each small triangle is.
- ◆ Substitute a blue block for two of the green blocks in the large triangle. Have children confirm that the blue block—since it is equivalent to two of the green triangles—is two-fourths, or one-half, of the triangle.

On Their Own

> *Can you solve these Pattern Block fraction puzzles?*
>
> - Working with a partner, use Pattern Blocks to solve each of these fraction puzzles in at least two different ways:
>
>   **Puzzle 1:** Build a triangle that is one-third green and two-thirds red.
>
>   **Puzzle 2:** Build a triangle that is two-thirds red, one-ninth green, and two-ninths blue.
>
>   **Puzzle 3:** Build a parallelogram that is three-fourths blue and one-fourth green.
>
>   **Puzzle 4:** Build a parallelogram that is two-thirds blue and one-third green.
>
> - Record and color each of your solutions on triangle paper and cut them out. Label the back of each solution with the puzzle number.

The Bigger Picture

Thinking and Sharing

Divide the chalkboard or display board into four sections, labeling them *Puzzle 1*, *Puzzle 2*, and so on. Have each pair post its solutions beneath the appropriate headings.

Use prompts such as these to promote class discussion:

- What discoveries did you make as you solved the puzzles?

- What strategies did you use to find solutions?

- How many possible solutions do you think there are to each of the puzzles?

- How are the solutions for each puzzle the same? How are they different?

- How can you convince us that a particular solution is correct?

Extending the Activity

1. Have children work with their partners to create their own fraction puzzles with triangles or parallelograms. Tell them to trace and color two possible solutions for each puzzle, and write the puzzle itself on the other side of the paper. Encourage children to share puzzles, perhaps in a "class puzzle book" or "class puzzle box" to be used at an independent math center.

2. Have children create puzzles in which a square or a hexagon represents the whole.

Where's the Mathematics?

In searching for solutions to the puzzles, children recognize that the relationships that exist among the areas of the Pattern Blocks play an important role. For example, in building shapes that are red and green, children need to use the fact that a red trapezoid is equivalent to three green triangles. Furthermore, they need to see that when a red trapezoid and a green triangle are adjoined to make a shape, the green triangle represents one-fourth of the area of the new shape (not one-third, as some children may incorrectly reason).

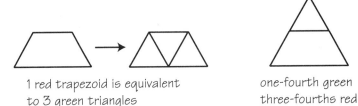

1 red trapezoid is equivalent
to 3 green triangles

one-fourth green
three-fourths red

As children examine and discuss one another's solutions, they will discover that some solutions look different but are, in one sense, really the same. For example, each of the solutions below shows a parallelogram that is three-fourths blue and one-fourth green.

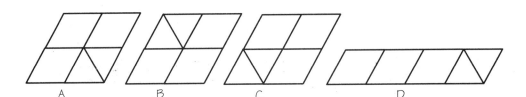

All of the solutions shown are made using the same combinations of blocks. In addition, Figures A, B, and C show solutions that are exactly the same size and shape. Solutions A and B are rotations of each other; however, the arrangement of blocks in Figure C is different from the arrangement used in A and B. Children may decide that Figures A and B are really the same solution. Some may decide that Figure C also represents the same solution as A and B because the size, shape, and components of the parallelogram in C are the same as those in A and B. Solution D, although composed of the same blocks as the other solutions, shows how the blocks can be arranged to form a different parallelogram that is also a solution.

Many children may work chiefly by trial and error, putting together blocks to create the large shape and then calculating and adjusting to make each color the correct fractional part of the whole shape. Children may, for example, if they have solved Puzzle 1 using three triangles and two trapezoids, substitute a third trapezoid for the triangles to show that the triangles make up one-third of the shape. Other children, using the triangle as a basic unit, might explain that the entire shape is equivalent to nine triangles; three triangles being three-ninths, or one-third of the whole shape.

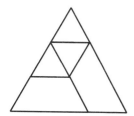 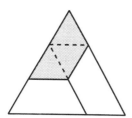 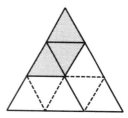

Children may discover that the ratio of blocks used for all solutions to a particular puzzle must be the same. For example, the solution shown above for Puzzle 1 shows that there must be three green triangles for every two red trapezoids in order for the triangle to be one-third green and two-thirds red. With this in mind, children may try to build triangles using combinations of blocks having this same ratio—six green triangles and four red trapezoids, nine green triangles and six red trapezoids, and so on.

Another helpful discovery that children may make concerns the number of green blocks needed to make triangles that are progressively bigger. One green block is, of course, the smallest possible Pattern Block triangle. The next Pattern Block triangle that is possible to build requires 4 green triangles or their equivalent; the one after that requires 9; then 16, 25, 36, and so on. Children may recognize these numbers as perfect squares. Since the triangle puzzles refer to fractional parts that are thirds and ninths, triangles made from the equivalent of, for example, 16 green triangles will not produce solutions since 16 cannot be divided evenly into thirds and ninths. Recognition of this may help children to see that the next largest triangle that will work will be one that is equivalent in size to 36 green triangles. Specifically, for Puzzle 1, this triangle would consist of 12 green triangles and 8 red trapezoids, and solutions for Puzzle 2 would consist of 4 green triangles, 8 red trapezoids, and 4 blue parallelograms.

Children may realize that the number of solutions to these puzzles is limited only by the number of blocks they have. Their understanding of the relationships involved may help them to see how to use proportional reasoning to generalize about additional solutions to these puzzles and to solve other problems involving fractional parts.

HOW MANY ANGLES?

- Angles
- Properties of geometric figures
- Spatial visualization

Getting Ready

What You'll Need

Pattern Blocks, several of each shape per child

Overhead Pattern Blocks (optional)

Overview

Children investigate the different angles that can be built using Pattern Blocks. In this activity, children have the opportunity to:

- build angles by adjoining smaller angles
- identify angles of various sizes, including those with measurements greater than 180°
- search for ways to know that all possible solutions to a problem have been found

The Activity

Before doing this activity, children should have successfully completed Pattern Block Angles, page 66, or should have a good understanding of angle measurement.

Introducing

- Review what children know about the angles of the Pattern Blocks.
- Ask them to show the smallest angle they can with a Pattern Block. All should agree that this is the 30° angle of the tan rhombus.
- Have children combine the tan rhombus with a different Pattern Block and figure out the measure of the new angle they have formed. Invite a few children to show their new angle and explain how they determined its measure.

90°

120°

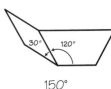

150°

On Their Own

How many different angles can you build with Pattern Blocks?

- Working with your partner, find all the different possible angles you can show using a single Pattern Block or any combination of Pattern Blocks.

- Record each solution by tracing the blocks and labeling the angle you have found with both the measurements of the individual angles (if you used more than one) and the measurement of the new angle.

- Be ready to explain how you know you've found all possible angles.

The Bigger Picture

Thinking and Sharing

Ask children to tell what angle measures they were able to find and list them on the chalkboard. If there is disagreement about any of the measures, have children work together to resolve the discrepancy.

Use prompts such as these to promote class discussion:

- What was the largest angle you found?

- Did you find that there was more than one way to build some of the angles? If so, explain why this was possible.

- What strategies did you use for finding new angles?

- What do you notice about the measures of the angles you were able to build?

- How did you decide you had found all the possible angles?

- What other discoveries did you make?

Extending the Activity

Ask different groups of children to find all the possible ways to build an angle with a particular measure using their Pattern Blocks. For example, one group might try to build angles measuring 120°, another might try to build angles measuring 150°, and so on. Have children record their work and use it for a class display.

Where's the Mathematics?

Children will find that there are numerous ways to build many of the angles. They may begin their search by randomly adjoining different blocks. However, as they continue to find new angles and record their measures, they may notice that the angles they have built all have measures that are multiples of 30°. This may help children by directing their search for new angles. Children should find that it is possible to make angles with measures of all the multiples of 30°, from 30° to 360°.

Be sure children understand that it is the design of the Pattern Blocks that limits the types of angles that can be built.

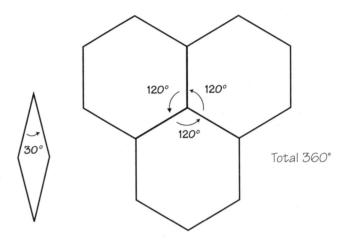

As children work with the blocks, they may notice some interesting relationships among the angles of the blocks and how they fit together. They also may learn to recognize properties of some of the kinds of angles they make, specifically those that measure 180° or larger. Children may notice that the outer edges of blocks put together to form an angle measuring 180° form a straight line.

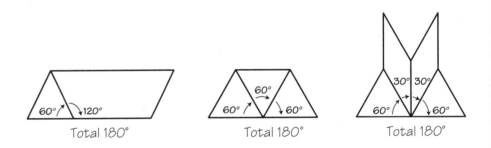

They also will find that they can build angles that measure more than 180°. For some children, this may be their first experience with these kinds of angles. Children may point out that when the Pattern Blocks are arranged to produce an angle that measures more than 180°, another angle—one measuring less than 180°—is also formed in what they may describe as the "empty space." Some children may realize that the measure of this other angle is the difference between 360° and the measure of the Pattern Block angle.

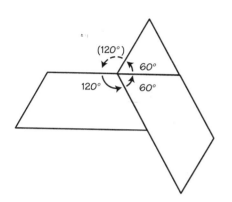

Total of Pattern Block angles 240°

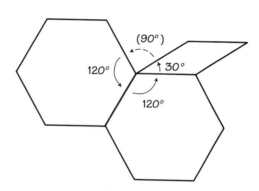

Total of Pattern Block angles 270°

Children may offer different explanations as to how they know that they have found all the possible angles that can be made. Partners who went about forming the angles in some systematic way may describe that they've exhausted all possible combinations of blocks. Others may say that as time went on, the new angles they formed continued to be equal in measure to angles they had already found. Children who noticed the pattern in the measures of the angles may feel convinced that they have found all the different angles once they have built angles with measures of every multiple of 30° between 30° and 360°. No matter how they conducted their search, or how many angles they found, children's experience with this activity will help provide a strong foundation for their work with angles in geometry.

HOW MANY CAN SIT?

- Perimeter
- Organizing and interpreting data
- Using patterns

Getting Ready

What You'll Need

Pattern Blocks, 1 set per pair
Overhead Pattern Blocks (optional)

Overview

Children use Pattern Blocks to investigate how perimeter changes as blocks are added to a shape. In this activity, children have the opportunity to:

- organize data
- recognize and use patterns to make predictions
- make generalizations

The Activity

Introducing

- Ask children to imagine that a green Pattern Block is a table and that each edge can seat one person. Ask them to think about how many people could sit at this table.

- Have children put two triangles together, each sharing one side with the other. Ask how many could sit at this new table.

- Next, ask children to predict how many can sit at a table made of three triangles lined up so that one side of the new triangle touches one side of the previous table. Tell children to build this new table and check their prediction.

- Show children how to make a chart to record what they have found:

Number of small tables (blocks)	Number that can sit
1	3
2	4
3	5

On Their Own

Can you predict how many people could sit at 100 tables?

- Working with a partner, pretend that a green Pattern Block is a table, and that bigger tables can be made by joining smaller tables.

- Build tables with triangles, and record on a chart how many people can sit at each bigger table. Build your tables in such a way that each time a new triangle is added it shares one side with the existing table.

- Continue until you have built at least 6 or 7 different tables.

- Look for a pattern in the numbers you record. Use the pattern to predict how many people can sit at a table built from 100 triangles.

- Build other tables, first using squares, then hexagons, and then pentagons. (For pentagons, join a square and a triangle to make each single table.) Be sure that one side of each new shape shares one side of the existing table.

- In each case, look for a pattern so you can predict how many people can sit at a table built from 100 single tables.

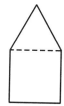

Pentagon table

The Bigger Picture

Thinking and Sharing

Invite children to share their charts and discuss their findings and predictions.

Use prompts such as these to promote class discussion:

- How many people can sit at 100 triangular tables? Explain how you know this.

- How many people can sit at 100 square tables? 100 pentagonal tables? 100 hexagonal tables? How do you know?

- What patterns did you find in the numbers you recorded?

- Why do you think each pattern grows in the way that it does?

Writing

Tell children to use words, pictures, charts, and/or numbers to explain what they would do to determine the number of people that could sit at 100 tables of any shape.

Extending the Activity

1. Have children repeat the activity using decagons formed by adjoining two hexagons. Ask them to make tables in which the decagons share one side, share two sides, and share three sides. Have them record their results and look for patterns.

Where's the Mathematics?

As children build new tables and count their sides, they begin to see how the growth of the perimeter of a shape is related to the way the shape grows geometrically. For example, as they join together triangles to make tables, children find that the perimeter increases by 1 unit each time a triangle is connected to the existing shape. This may surprise children who may think that the perimeter should increase by 3 units since a triangle has three sides. Other children may think the perimeter should increase by 2 units since one of the sides of the new triangle will end up interior to the new shape. As they continue to "grow" the shape, children may come to see that each new triangle takes away an existing seat at the table and adds 2 more, resulting in an increase of only 1 seat.

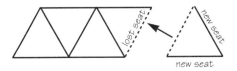

Just as each added triangle makes room for one more person at the table, each added square makes room for two more people, each added pentagon makes room for three more people, and each added hexagon makes room for four more people.

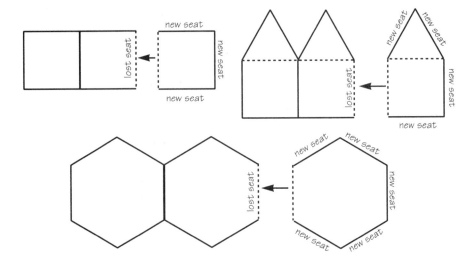

Children may use different methods for finding the number of people that can sit at the tables made from 100 single tables. Some children may base their predictions on patterns they see in the numbers in their chart. They

2. Challenge children to use the smallest number of Pattern Blocks they can to make a table that will seat exactly 10 people. Then have them do the same for tables that will seat exactly 15 people, exactly 20 people, and exactly 25 people. Have them discuss their findings and make a generalization.

may continue the patterns, by adding the common difference to find the 100th term in each sequence, or they may be able to make a connection between the number of tables used and the number of seats that are created. For example, in studying the chart below, children may notice that the number of people that can sit at a table made from pentagons is 3 times the number of pentagons plus 2. From there, they can figure out how many people can sit at a table made from 100 pentagons simply by applying this formula.

Number of pentagons (tables)	Number of people who can sit
1	5
2	8
3	11
4	14
5	17
6	20
7	23

Other children may make predictions based on patterns they see in the actual formation of the Pattern Block "tables." For example, some children may notice that when squares are joined in straight lines to make tables, each square in the arrangement provides a seat for two people (one on either side of the table), with the squares at the end providing two additional seats (at the heads of the table). These children may realize that they can figure out the number of seats for any table constructed this way by multiplying 2 times the number of squares and adding 2.

 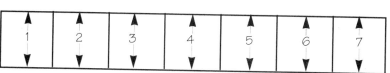

7 squares
(7 x 2) + 2 = 16

It is likely that not all children will be able to generalize their findings. However, it is valuable for children to share their insights and strategies with each other. In doing so, children discover different ways of looking at problems and interpreting results.

LOOKING FOR SYMMETRY

- Symmetry
- Properties of geometric figures
- Spatial visualization

Getting Ready

What You'll Need

Pattern Blocks, about 20 blue, 20 green, and 2 of each of the other shapes per pair

Mirrors, 1 per pair

Pattern Block triangle paper, page 90

Crayons

Scissors

Overhead Pattern Blocks (optional)

Overview

Children check individual Pattern Blocks for symmetry, then create designs that meet various criteria relating to symmetry. In this activity, children have the opportunity to:

- recognize both line and rotational symmetry in shapes and designs
- develop strategies for checking for symmetry
- sort and classify designs based on the types of symmetry they possess

The Activity

You may want to show children how to use a mirror to check for line symmetry. Have them stand a mirror on top of the shape, move it to a location that they think may be a line of symmetry, and look to see if the half of the shape showing, together with its mirror image, looks like the whole shape.

Introducing

- Ask children to tell what it means to say that a shape has *symmetry*. Discuss the idea of symmetry as a kind of balance that a shape has.

- Explain that a line of symmetry is a line that can be drawn somewhere on the shape in such a way that if the shape could be folded on this line, the part on one side of the line would fit exactly on top of the part on the other side of the line.

- Hold up the orange Pattern Block and ask children how many lines of symmetry it has. Establish that the orange square has four lines of symmetry.

- Demonstrate rotational symmetry using two square overhead Pattern Blocks. Place the blocks side-by-side, and mark a small dot in the same corner of each of the squares. Then rotate one square clockwise, stopping at each point at which the square's orientation is the same as the other square's (every 1/4 of a turn).

On Their Own

Can you build Pattern Block designs that have different kinds of symmetry?

- Working with a partner, check each of the Pattern Blocks for both line symmetry and rotational symmetry. You may want to use a mirror to help check for lines of symmetry.

- Record your findings.

- Now build designs using 4 blue blocks and 4 green blocks. Try to make designs that have 1 line of symmetry; 2 lines of symmetry; rotational symmetry; no symmetry.

- Record each design on triangle paper.

- Color each design to match the Pattern Blocks, and then cut it out.

The Bigger Picture

Thinking and Sharing

Have children talk about the individual Pattern Blocks, telling how many lines of symmetry each has and whether or not each has rotational symmetry. Invite one pair of children to post one of their designs. Then ask all children who think that their designs have the same type of symmetry as the one posted to post their designs with this first design. Have children look at the posted designs and discuss whether or not they belong together. When agreement is reached on the first set of postings, have another pair of children post another design. Continue the process until all designs are posted.

Use prompts such as these to promote class discussion:

- How did you check your Pattern Blocks for line symmetry?
- How many lines of symmetry does each block have?
- How did you check your Pattern Blocks for rotational symmetry?
- At what fraction of a rotation does each block have rotational symmetry?
- How did you go about building designs that have certain kinds of symmetry?
- How can you prove your designs have line symmetry? rotational symmetry?

Writing

Have children write about which blue and green Pattern Block design was hardest to make, and why.

Extending the Activity

Have children use a variety of Pattern Blocks to build designs with different numbers of lines of symmetry or with different amounts of rotational symmetry. Children can sort, post, and discuss their designs.

Where's the Mathematics?

Some children will find it fairly easy to look at shapes and be able to tell if they have line symmetry. Others may need to verify their ideas by using mirrors or by tracing around shapes, cutting out the tracings, and folding them. Children may be surprised to discover how many lines of symmetry some of the blocks possess.

Children should find that each individual block has at least one line of symmetry. The square has four, the triangle has three, the blue parallelogram and tan rhombus each have two, the trapezoid has one, and the hexagon has six, as shown.

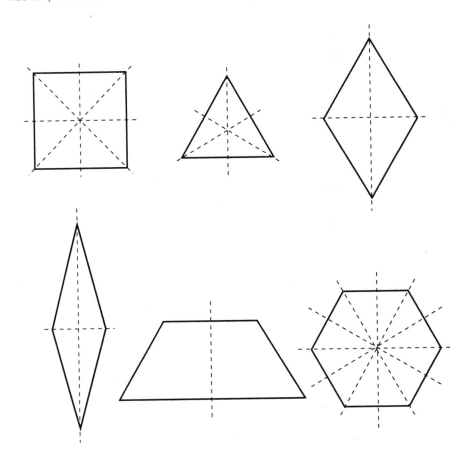

To check for rotational symmetry, some children may need only work with one block at a time, turning it to see whether different rotations of the block look the same. Other children may need to work with two of each block, leaving one stationary while turning the other. It may be difficult for some children to recognize what fractional part of a rotation produces the symmetry. These children may benefit from using a pair of blocks with one corner of each marked (as described in the *Introducing* activity), and/or from rotating the block inside a drawn circle, tracing the arc of the rotation as they turn the block.

Through their exploration, children should find that every block except the trapezoid has rotational symmetry. The triangle has symmetry after each one-third of a rotation (120°), the square after each one-fourth of rotation (90°), the blue parallelogram and tan rhombus after one-half of a rotation (180°), and the hexagon after each one-sixth of a rotation (60°).

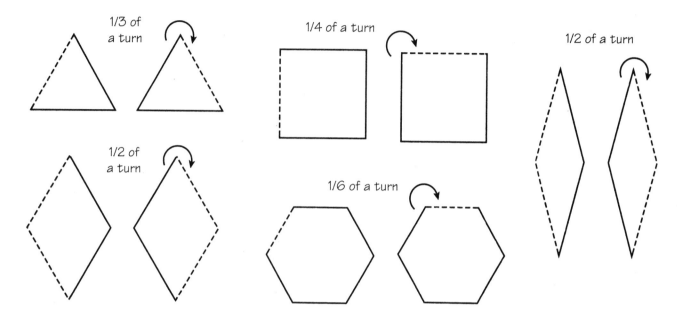

Children may make a wide variety of interesting designs that exhibit different kinds of symmetry. They may find that they need to alter some of their designs if they want them to have *only* the kind of symmetry described. Children may find it especially challenging to make a design that has rotational symmetry but no lines of symmetry. An example of such a design is shown below.

If no group builds a design that has only rotational symmetry, you may want to challenge them to try to create such a design.

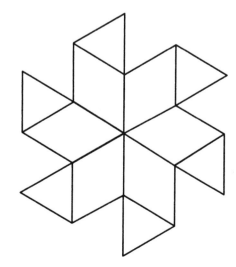

PATTERN BLOCK ANGLES

- Angles
- Estimation
- Spatial visualization
- Problem solving strategies

Getting Ready

What You'll Need

Pattern Blocks, several of each shape per pair

Hinged mirrors (optional)

Overview

Children investigate the angles of each Pattern Block shape. In this activity, children have the opportunity to:

- ◆ create strategies for measuring angles
- ◆ develop their understanding of the size of an angle as a measurement of rotation
- ◆ figure fractional parts of a whole
- ◆ use the language of geometry

The Activity

So that children will be able to talk about the different angles of the blocks, be sure they know that a 90° angle is called a right angle, that any angle wider than a right angle is called an obtuse angle, and that any angle smaller than a right angle is called an acute angle.

Introducing

- ◆ Use the classroom clock to remind children that the size of an angle is a measurement of rotation and is measured in degrees.
- ◆ Confirm that a clock hand that moves from the 12, all the way around the clock and back to the 12, has rotated 360°, the number of degrees in a circle.
- ◆ Have children identify a 180° and a 90° angle by figuring out how far a clock hand has rotated if it moves halfway around the clock, and how far it has rotated if it moves from the 12 to the 3.
- ◆ To reinforce children's ability to recognize angles and to determine their measures, ask them to find the measure of the angle formed by the hands of a clock when the time is two o'clock. Ask children to explain how they got their answers.

On Their Own

Can you figure out the measures of the angles of each of the Pattern Block shapes?

- Working with your partner, look at each Pattern Block and estimate the measurement of the angle at each corner. Keep a record of your estimates.

- Now find a way to figure out the number of degrees in each angle.

- You can use the blocks themselves to figure out the angle measures, or you can use the hinged mirrors. Here's how to use the mirrors:

  1. Place a corner of the block in the hinged mirrors.

  2. Close the mirrors until the corner nestles snugly between them.

  3. Use other blocks to build what you see in the mirrors.

  4. Calculate the number of degrees in the nestled corner by dividing 360° by the number of blocks you used to build the design formed by the block and its reflection.

- Record your measurements next to your estimates.

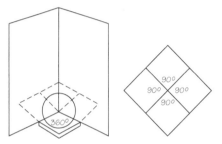

The Bigger Picture

Thinking and Sharing

Invite children to share their results. If there are disagreements, allow children to work together to resolve them.

Use prompts such as these to promote class discussion:

- What strategies did you use to figure out the measures of the angles?

- What discoveries did you make?

- Which blocks have only congruent angles (angles that are all the same size)? What are the measures of the angles in each of these shapes?

- Which block has only acute angles? only obtuse angles?

- What are the measures of the angles of the trapezoid? the blue parallelogram? the tan rhombus?

- Were the measures of some angles harder to figure out than others? Why?

- How did your estimates compare with the actual measures of the angles?

- Why does dividing 360° by the total number of blocks you see give the measure of the angle at the corner nestled in the mirrors?

Extending the Activity

1. Have children investigate relationships among the angles of the Pattern Blocks. Ask them to find combinations of blocks whose angles are equal in size to each of the angles of the individual blocks. (For example, the angle of the hexagon, 120°, can be formed by adjoining an angle from a square and an angle from a tan rhombus.)

Where's the Mathematics?

As they work through this exploration activity, children discover how the angles of the various Pattern Block shapes are related, and learn why the blocks fit together in certain ways.

Children will find that the square, the triangle, and the hexagon are the only shapes that have angles that are all congruent. All of the other shapes have both acute and obtuse angles. The measures of the angles of the square will most likely be the easiest for children to identify, as they are right (90°) angles. From there, children may check the other shapes to see if they contain any right angles. When they find that they do not, children may then check to see if two or more of the same size angle fit together to form a right angle. Children will find that for all of the angles except the small angle of the tan rhombus, two angles of the same size, when adjoined, form an angle that is larger than a right angle. Children may discover, however, that *three* of the small angles of the tan rhombus can be adjoined to form a right angle, thus revealing that the measure of this smallest angle is 30° (90° ÷ 3).

Once the measure of the small angle of the tan rhombus has been established, children may try using it to determine the measures of other angles. For example, some children may see that two of these small angles fit into a corner of the triangle; thus, the measure of each angle of the triangle is 60°. Since the angles of the triangle are congruent to the acute angles of both the trapezoid and the blue parallelogram, children can conclude that these angles also measure 60°. Furthermore, since when two triangles are put together, adjoining angles form an angle congruent to an angle of the hexagon, the obtuse angle of the blue parallelogram, and the obtuse angle of the trapezoid, these angles must each measure 120°. Finally, children will need to use a combination of some of the angle measures they found to determine the measure of the obtuse angle of the tan rhombus. Angles congruent to this angle can be formed several ways, such as by adjoining an angle of a square and the acute angle of a blue parallelogram, or by adjoining an angle of a hexagon and an acute angle of a tan rhombus, or even by adjoining five acute angles of tan rhombuses. Each of these arrangements establishes that the measure of the obtuse angle of the tan rhombus is 150°.

---

2. Have children use hinged mirrors to figure out the total number of degrees in two adjoining angles from two different shapes.

3. Ask children to total the measures of the angles of each of the Pattern Block shapes. Ask them to investigate further to see what generalization they can make about the sum of the angle measures of a quadrilateral.

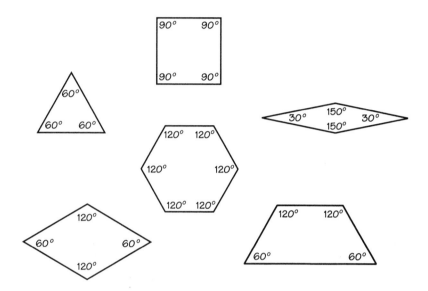

Some children may prefer to use the hinged mirror to figure out the measures of the angles. In building what they see in the mirrors, children should find that the interior angles where the blocks all meet form one complete rotation of 360°. Since the individual angles are all congruent to each other, children can calculate the measure of one of the angles by dividing 360° by the total number of blocks.

The only angle for which the hinged-mirror method will not work, is the obtuse angle of the tan rhombus. Children will find that its reflection does not show a whole number of blocks. To find the measure of this angle, children will need to use a different method, such as the one described above involving the construction of a congruent angle using two or more blocks whose angle measures are known, or perhaps by building an arrangement of different blocks, such as the one shown here, in which the angles at the point where the blocks all meet form one complete rotation of 360°. Using this configuration and the fact that the measure of the angle of the triangle is 60°, children can determine the measure of one obtuse angle by subtracting 60° from 360°, and dividing by 2.

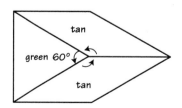

PATTERN BLOCK RIDDLES

NUMBER • GEOMETRY • MEASUREMENT • LOGIC
- Deductive reasoning
- Fractions
- Percents
- Properties of geometric figures
- Area
- Perimeter

Getting Ready

What You'll Need

Pattern Blocks, about 30 per pair

Paper bags stapled shut, labeled *Riddle 1, Riddle 2, Riddle 3, Riddle 4,* and *Riddle 5*, containing the following Pattern Blocks:

Riddle 1: 3 yellow, 2 blue, 2 green
Riddle 2: 2 yellow, 1 red, 6 blue
Riddle 3: 1 yellow, 2 red, 4 blue, 1 green
Riddle 4: 2 blue, 2 green
Riddle 5: 1 red, 1 orange

Overview

Children identify hidden collections of Pattern Blocks by solving descriptive clues. In this activity, children have the opportunity to:

- use deductive reasoning
- work with fractions and percents
- compare areas of geometric shapes
- use the language of mathematics

Can you solve this riddle?
I have hidden 5 Pattern Blocks.
The 3 smallest blocks exactly cover the largest block.
One of the blocks covers $\frac{2}{3}$ of the largest block.

The Activity

Introducing

- Hide one red, one blue, and three green Pattern Blocks in a bag or behind your back.

- Tell children you have hidden some Pattern Blocks. Explain that you will give clues so they can figure out what blocks you have hidden.

- Present the sample riddle below, one clue at a time. After each clue, ask children what they know about the solution so far.

    Sample Riddle
    I have hidden five Pattern Blocks.
    The three smallest blocks exactly cover the largest block.
    One of the blocks covers two-thirds of the largest block.

- After children have given their solutions and explanations, reveal your Pattern Blocks.

On Their Own

Can you solve these riddles and figure out what Pattern Blocks are in the bags?

- Each of the riddles below contains clues to Pattern Blocks hidden in different paper bags.

- Work with your partner to solve each riddle. Record your solutions.

Riddle 1

The area of all the blocks in the bag together is the same as the area of 24 green triangles.

Three of the blocks together make up 75% of the total area.

The green blocks cover one-half as much area as the blue blocks.

Riddle 2

There are 9 blocks in the bag.

The area covered by the yellow blocks is equal to the area covered by the blue blocks.

The area covered by the red block is one-eighth the area covered by the yellow and blue blocks combined.

Riddle 3

There are 8 blocks in the bag.

50% are blocks that would each cover one-third of the largest block.

25% are blocks that would each cover one-half of the largest block.

The bag contains red, blue, green, and yellow blocks.

Riddle 4

The blocks in the bag can be arranged to cover a yellow hexagon.

They can also be arranged to make a parallelogram.

There are only 2 colors of blocks in the bag.

There are no red blocks.

Riddle 5

There are 2 blocks in the bag.

The blocks can be arranged to make a hexagon.

This hexagon has 2 right angles.

The perimeter of this hexagon is 7 units. (1 unit = the length of a side of a green triangle).

The Bigger Picture

Thinking and Sharing

Ask volunteers to share their answers with the class. If children disagree on any of the solutions, allow time for them to work to resolve the disagreements. Give children the opportunity to explain how they know their solutions are correct. Finally, reveal the contents of each bag.

Use prompts such as these to promote class discussion:

- What discoveries did you make while solving the riddles?

- How did you go about solving the riddles?

- Do you think your solution for each riddle is the only possible solution? How can you prove that?

- Was there a riddle that was especially hard to solve? Which one, and why?

Extending the Activity

1. Have children work with partners to write their own Pattern Block riddles. Suggest they first choose the blocks and then make up clues that can lead others to discover their combination of blocks. Children could write their clues on a 3 by 5 card and clip the card to a paper bag

Teacher Talk

Where's the Mathematics?

Riddles, such as the ones in this activity, involve children in using mathematical language to describe relationships and mathematical properties. As they read and interpret the clues, children focus on the attributes of the various shapes and the ways in which the shapes relate to each other. They use mathematical language to express their thoughts and hypotheses.

Children also use logical reasoning as they work through the riddles, adjusting their selection of blocks to fit the various clues. For example, after reading the first two clues in Riddle 2, children may deduce that the bag might contain 1 yellow block and 3 blue blocks (among other blocks), or 2 yellow blocks and 6 blue blocks (among other blocks). The third clue helps children to reason that the latter must be the case, as the area of yellow and blue blocks together must be 8 times the area of the red block.

This activity also affords an opportunity to reinforce the concepts of fractions and percents. The clues incorporate fractions and percents in comparisons based on area. In working with these clues, children see how fractions and percents can be used to describe relationships and provide comparative information.

To solve the riddles, some children may find it easier to work with one clue at a time, selecting combinations of blocks that fit the first clue, and

containing the blocks. Challenge children to write the fewest number of clues necessary for their riddle. You may wish to limit the number of blocks children may use.

2. Challenge children to write Pattern Block riddles that have multiple solutions.

adjusting the selection to fit each of the following clues as they work through the riddle. Other children may prefer to read through the entire riddle and search for combinations of blocks that seem to satisfy all of the clues, verifying their solution by checking the final combination against each clue.

For a variety of reasons, some children may find some riddles more difficult to solve than others. For example, the fact that Riddles 1 and 4 do not specify the number of blocks in the bag may make some children feel these riddles are tricky. Children who are not yet comfortable with the concept of percent may find Riddle 3 to be difficult since the main clues both involve percents. Some children may find Riddle 5 to be challenging especially if they limit their conception of a hexagon to only regular hexagons. These children may need to be reminded that any 6-sided polygon is a hexagon. To solve Riddle 5, children will also need to remember that the longest side of the trapezoid block is twice as long as the sides of the other Pattern Blocks.

Most children enjoy solving riddles and explaining how they solved them. Their explanations often provide clues to the ways that they think and reason. The development of these deductive reasoning skills is important in children's growth as problem solvers.

REACH INTO THE BAG

- **Properties of geometric figures**
- **Spatial visualization**
- **Angles**

Getting Ready

What You'll Need

Paper lunch bags, 1 per group, containing several Pattern Blocks of each shape

Overview

Children identify Pattern Blocks that fit specific descriptions, using only their sense of touch. In this activity, children have the opportunity to:

- ◆ investigate the attributes of Pattern Block shapes
- ◆ discover that different shapes share certain characteristics
- ◆ use the language of geometry
- ◆ find multiple solutions to a problem

The Activity

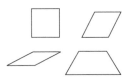

Pattern Blocks that are quadrilaterals.

Introducing

- ◆ Hold out a bag containing several of each kind of Pattern Block. Ask a child to reach into the bag, and, without looking, pick out a shape that is a quadrilateral and show it to the class.

- ◆ Invite another child to reach into the bag and pick out a different shape that is a quadrilateral and show it to the class.

- ◆ Ask the children to explain how they selected the shapes they picked.

On Their Own

Can you reach into a bag of Pattern Blocks, and—without looking—find shapes that fit specific descriptions?

- Working with your group, take turns reaching into your bag and picking out a block that fits the first description on the list below. Keep searching to find all the different-shaped blocks that fit. Remember... no peeking!

- Record the blocks you picked.

- Now search to find blocks that fit each of the other descriptions on the list. Be sure to return the blocks to the bag after each search, and to record the blocks you picked for each description. Sometimes there will only be one block; often there will be more than one.

DESCRIPTIONS

1. a block that has no right angles

2. a block that has right angles

3. a block with all sides equal (an equilateral shape)

4. a block with only obtuse angles

5. a block that is 6 times as large as the smallest block

6. a block with both acute and obtuse angles

7. a block with only acute angles

8. the block with the second longest perimeter

9. the block with the smallest angle

10. the block with the largest area

11. a block with exactly 2 lines of symmetry

The Bigger Picture

Thinking and Sharing

Invite volunteers to offer solutions for each description. Encourage children to discuss and settle any disagreements they may have.

Use prompts such as these to promote class discussion:

- What kinds of things were easy to identify by touch? What kinds of things were harder?

- How were you able to identify right, acute, and obtuse angles without looking?

- What did you feel for to find an equilateral shape?

- How could you tell whether a block had two lines of symmetry?

- How would you describe the way different shapes feel?

Writing

Ask children to describe the things they were able to find out about the blocks just by feeling them.

Where's the Mathematics?

As they search through their bags of Pattern Blocks, children focus on the physical attributes of the shapes through their sense of touch. They learn to identify what geometric concepts such as acute angles, right angles, and perimeter "feel like." They also learn to relate the geometric language to the characteristics of the shapes.

Some children may feel sure that they know which descriptions will have only one solution and which will have more than one. As they compare the different blocks they select, children recognize that different shapes may share many of the same attributes. For example, the trapezoid, the blue parallelogram, and the tan rhombus all have both acute and obtuse angles (#6).

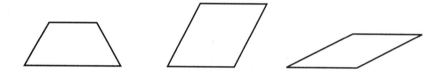

Children may talk about different kinds of angles according to the way that the angles feel to them. In searching for a block that has only acute angles (#7), children may say that they searched for a shape that was "very pointy" at all of its corners (the triangle); whereas, when searching for a shape that has only obtuse angles (#4), they may say they were feeling for corners that were dull (the hexagon).

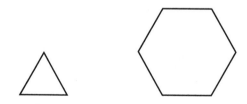

Extending the Activity

Have children work in small groups to write their own list of descriptions for blocks to be found by reaching into a bag. Each group should write 10 descriptions. Have groups exchange lists and try to find all the blocks that fit each description.

In describing how they worked on description #8, children may say they tried to compare perimeters by feeling around the edges of the shapes. Many children may know from their past experience with Pattern Blocks that the hexagon has the greatest perimeter, and may need only to compare the perimeters of two or three of the remaining shapes to see which has the next largest perimeter (the trapezoid). Their past experience, and the fact that the hexagon is the heaviest piece, may lead children to select it as the block with the largest area (#10).

In working on description #3, children may first identify only the triangle and/or the square blocks as solutions. Further investigation should lead them to see that all of the blocks except the trapezoid are equilateral.

Some children may have difficulty finding blocks that have exactly two lines of symmetry (#11). They may pull out a square or a trapezoid, thinking that these shapes are solutions. It may be helpful for them to trace these shapes onto paper and test them for lines of symmetry using paper-folding or a mirror. Children should find that only the blue parallelogram and the tan rhombus have exactly two lines of symmetry.

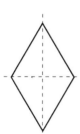 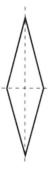

SQUARE AND TRIANGULAR NUMBERS

- Organizing and interpreting data
- Pattern recognition
- Spatial visualization

Getting Ready

What You'll Need

Pattern Blocks, 1 set per pair
Overhead Pattern Blocks (optional)

Overview

Children use Pattern Blocks to build increasingly larger squares and triangles and examine the underlying number patterns. In this activity, children have the opportunity to:

- learn the characteristics of square and triangular numbers
- recognize patterns
- make predictions based on patterns

The Activity

Introducing

- Ask children to show a square with one Pattern Block.
- Have children use orange blocks to make the next bigger square.
- Set up a table such as the following on the chalkboard, and have children record what they have done.

Square	Number of blocks added	Total number of blocks
1st	1	1
2nd	3	4

- Now show the green triangle and model how you want children to build the next bigger triangle with green blocks as shown here.

- Point out that in building bigger triangles, one new row is added to a side of the previous triangle, leaving spaces between blocks.

On Their Own

> **What patterns can you find in the numbers of Pattern Blocks that can be used to make squares and triangles?**
>
> - Using the orange blocks, work with your partner to build increasingly larger squares.
>
> - Record, each time, both the number of blocks you added to build the next bigger square, and the total number of blocks in the new square.
>
> - Record the numbers through the eighth square, but build squares only until you discover the pattern that will give you all the numbers you need.
>
> - Now use the green blocks to build increasingly bigger triangles.
>
> - Build new triangles by adding blocks to one side of the previous triangle. All blocks should be positioned the same way, and there should be spaces between all the blocks, as shown.
>
> - Record, each time, as you did with the squares, through the eighth triangle, but build only until you discover the pattern.
>
> - Be ready to discuss the patterns your tables reveal.

The Bigger Picture

Thinking and Sharing

Have children help you create class charts for both the squares and the triangles they made. If groups have data that differs, have children work together to reach agreement. Invite observations and discussion.

Use prompts such as these to promote class discussion:

- What patterns do you see in the squares table?
- How could you explain with the blocks why the numbers increase as they do?
- How many blocks would be needed for the tenth square? How do you know?
- What patterns do you see in the triangles table?
- How could you explain with the blocks why the numbers increase as they do?
- How many blocks would be needed for the tenth triangle? How do you know?

Writing

Ask children to write about the patterns that they discovered in the blocks and in their tables.

Extending the Activity

1. If a certain number of squares can be arranged to form a rectangle, that number is considered to be a rectangular number. For example, 6 is a rectangular number because six squares can be arranged in two rows of three to form a rectangle. (Note: One, and any other number for which the rectangle would only be one block wide, is not considered to be a

Where's the Mathematics?

As they build their squares and triangles and count the number of blocks, children are discovering square and triangular numbers. The square numbers through 64 appear in the third column of the table below.

Square	# of blocks added	Total # of blocks
1st	1	1
2nd	3	4
3rd	5	9
4th	7	16
5th	9	25
6th	11	36
7th	13	49
8th	15	64

Children may see several patterns in the tables they have made. For example, children may notice that in the second column above, all of the numbers are odd and they increase by 2 with each larger shape. They may also notice that for any square, the number of blocks added to the previous square plus all the numbers above this number in the table results in the number of total blocks in the new square. Children might correctly conclude that square numbers can always be figured by adding consecutive odd numbers beginning with 1. Some children might use this method to predict how many blocks are needed to build the tenth square, that is, they might add the first 10 odd numbers (1, 3, 5, 7, 9, 11, 13, 15, 17, and 19) to get 100.

As they build squares, children may also notice that the width and the height of a square are always the same, or that the number of blocks across the square is always the same as the number of blocks down the square. From their previous experiences with square and rectangular arrangements, children may recall that the number of blocks in the arrangement can be found by multiplying the number of blocks in each row by the number of rows (width times height). This may lead them to realize that square numbers can be found by multiplying a number by itself. Children are likely to use this insight to predict that the number of blocks in the tenth square is 10 x 10, or 100.

rectangular number.) Challenge children to use the orange Pattern Blocks to discover which numbers from 1 to 30 are rectangular numbers.

Remind children that squares are rectangles.

2. Have children identify those rectangular numbers from 1 through 30 that can be shown with two or more different rectangles, and build each possible rectangle.

Triangle	# of blocks added	Total # of blocks
1st	1	1
2nd	2	3
3rd	3	6
4th	4	10
5th	5	15
6th	6	21
7th	7	28
8th	8	36

The second column of the triangular number table is also revealing.

Here, children can see that with each new triangle, the number of blocks added is one larger than the previous number added. Children can notice that if it takes five more triangles to build the fifth triangle than to build the fourth triangle, then it will take six more triangles to build the sixth triangle. Children can also see that for any triangle, the number of blocks added to the previous triangle plus all the numbers above this number in the table is the total number of blocks in the new triangle. For example, if seven additional triangles are needed to build the seventh triangle, then adding seven plus all the numbers above it in the table will result in the total number of triangles needed to build the seventh triangle.

Looking at the blocks, children may see that the base of each successive triangle is 1 block longer than the base of the triangle before it.

3rd triangle

4th triangle

5th triangle

It follows that if the first triangle has a base of 1 block, the second will have a base of 2 blocks, so it will need 2 new triangles. The next triangle will have a base of 3 blocks, so 3 triangles will have to be added, and so on. Recognition of this visual pattern may enable children to reason that the tenth triangle will have a base of 10 blocks and, therefore, the total number of blocks needed to build it will be 1 + 2 + 3 + 4 + 5 + 6 + 7 + 8 + 9 + 10, or 55 blocks.

SURROUND

• **Organizing and interpreting data**
• **Using patterns**

Getting Ready

What You'll Need

Pattern Blocks, 1 set per group
Overhead Pattern Blocks (optional)

Overview

Children investigate the pattern of growth in the number of Pattern Blocks needed when one block is surrounded by blocks of the same kind and when each resulting design is then surrounded. In this activity, children have the opportunity to:

◆ discover patterns

◆ record data in a useful way

◆ use patterns to make predictions and solve problems

The Activity

Introducing

◆ Ask children to place one triangle in front of them.

◆ Ask how many triangles they think it will take to completely surround this triangle.

◆ Have children check their prediction by surrounding the triangle. Their results should look like this:

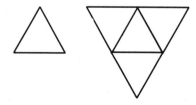

On Their Own

If you keep surrounding one kind of Pattern Block with Pattern Blocks of the same kind, can you predict how many blocks you'll need to make each new design?

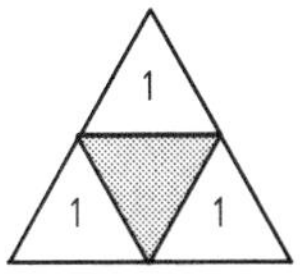

- Working with your group, surround 1 triangle with other triangles. Call this *Design 1*.

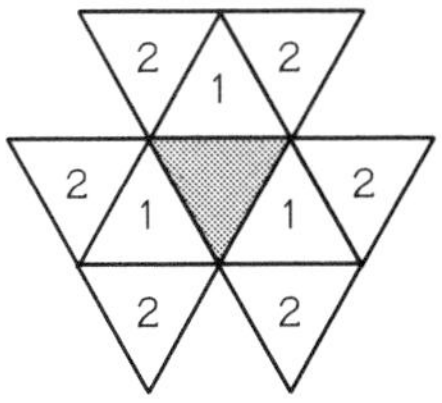

- Find a way to record your design. One way is to trace around it and mark it with numbers as shown at the right.

Design 1

- Next, surround each of the triangles in Design 1 with new triangles. Call this new design *Design 2*.

- Record the number of blocks you added to Design 1 to make Design 2.

Design 2

- Now predict how many triangles it will take to surround Design 2. Use triangles to check your prediction.

- Continue predicting, surrounding, and recording until you have built the sixth design.

- Predict how many blocks it will take to build the tenth design.

- Repeat the problem using the square, the blue parallelogram, the tan rhombus, and the hexagon.

- Now make a table that shows all your findings. Look for patterns in your results.

The Bigger Picture

Thinking and Sharing

Have children use their tables to discuss what they have discovered.

Use prompts such as these to promote class discussion:

- How many blocks did it take to surround the triangle (square, parallelogram, and so on) each time?

- Can you describe the pattern by which the number of blocks is growing?

- What relationship do you see between a block's shape and the growing pattern?

- How many blocks did you predict it would take to make each tenth design? How many do you think it would take to make each twentieth design?

- Can you explain why the numbers grow as they do?

Extending the Activity

Have children repeat the activity using the trapezoid. Tell them to match short edges to short edges and longer edges to longer edges. When they are done, have them discuss whether or not the trapezoid designs grow in the same way that the other shapes grow.

Where's the Mathematics?

Children will find that the number of sides of each shape determines how may blocks will be required to surround it the first time.

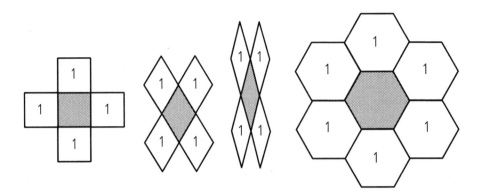

The second surrounding of the pattern will need twice as many blocks as the first; the third, three times as many, and so on.

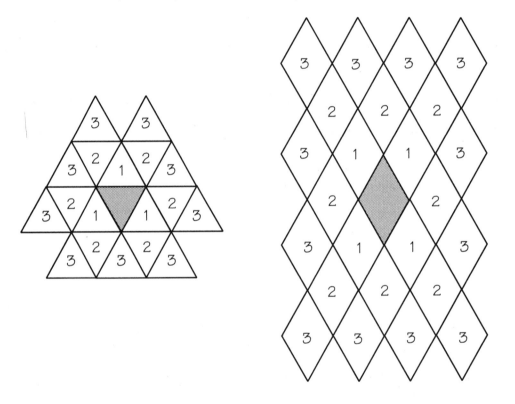

Once children notice the pattern in the way the number of blocks is increasing, they can continue their tables to find out how many blocks are needed for the tenth or twentieth or any other stage of the design. Some may also arrive at formulas for finding the number of blocks needed for larger designs. With the triangle, the number of the design multiplied by 3 tells how many blocks to add each time; with the four-sided figures, the number of the design multiplied by 4 tells how many new blocks to add; and with the hexagon, the number of the design multiplied by 6 results in the number of blocks to add.

Children may be able to discover why the numbers increase as they do. For example, when they surround the single triangle, each of the surrounding blocks covers one side of the first triangle but has two sides exposed. Children can see that it will take six triangles to surround those three triangles so that each of their two exposed sides is surrounded.

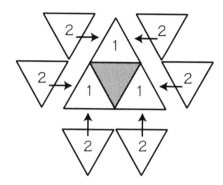

However, to surround triangle Design 2, there are three places where a single triangle will cover exposed sides of the two different triangles. Therefore, instead of needing 12 triangles (as children may predict), only 9 are needed.

Children will find that a similar situation occurs when surrounding the other shapes. For example, in surrounding square Design 1, although there are three exposed sides on each of the four squares used to surround the original square, squares placed in the four open corners of the design cover exposed sides of two squares. Therefore 8 (not 12) squares are needed to surround Design 1.

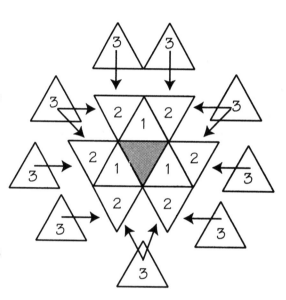

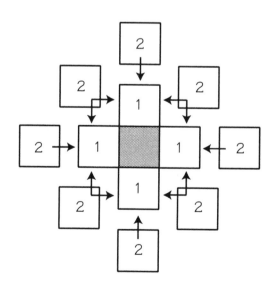

It is important for children to recognize the value of identifying patterns for use in solving problems. In this activity, as well as in other problem settings, it is often not practical to build the tenth, twentieth, or other large stage of a growing pattern. However, by finding and using patterns, information about these larger stages can be accurately predicted.

WHAT'S MY VALUE?

Getting Ready

What You'll Need

Pattern Blocks (no orange or tan), about 30 per pair

Pattern Block triangle paper, page 90

Crayons

Overhead Pattern Blocks (optional)

Overview

Given that a certain Pattern Block has a value of 1, children find the value of large Pattern Block designs. In this activity, children have the opportunity to:

- determine fractional parts
- recognize that fractional values are determined by the value of the whole
- calculate total value when the value of a unit is known

The Activity

Introducing

- Display a yellow hexagon and a green triangle.
- Ask children to work with a partner to find the value of the green triangle given that the value of the yellow hexagon is 1.
- Next, ask them to then figure out the values of a blue parallelogram and a red trapezoid when the value of the yellow hexagon is 1.
- Invite volunteers to share and explain their findings. Encourage them to use Pattern Blocks to support their explanations.

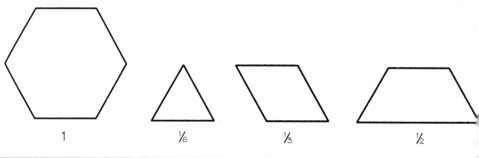

1   ⅙   ⅓   ½

On Their Own

> **How can you find the value of a large Pattern Block design when you know the value of 1 block?**
>
> - Working with a partner, create a Pattern Block design using 20-30 blocks of at least 3 different colors. Use only red, green, yellow, and blue blocks.
>
> - Draw your design on triangle paper and color it to match the blocks you used.
>
> - Figure out the value of your design if the hexagon equals 1. Write this number on the back of your paper.
>
> - Now figure out the value of your design if the trapezoid equals 1.
>
> - Finally, figure out the value of your design if the blue parallelogram equals 1.
>
> - Record each of these values on the back of your design.
>
> - Exchange designs with another pair and try to figure out the values of their design in each of the three situations (hexagon = 1, trapezoid = 1, and blue parallelogram = 1). If your results are different, work out the values together.

The Bigger Picture

Thinking and Sharing

Have children discuss how they figured out values and share any discoveries they may have made.

Use prompts such as these to promote class discussion:

- How did you figure out the value of the designs when the hexagon was 1? when the trapezoid was 1? when the blue parallelogram was 1?

- How did you determine fractional parts?

- Did you notice any patterns in the different values for your design? If so, what were they?

- How can you explain the patterns in the values?

Extending the Activity

Assign a certain Pattern Block a value of 1. Then challenge children to create a design with a predetermined value. For example, assign the hexagon a value of 1 and have children use a variety of blocks to create a design with a value of $24\frac{1}{3}$.

Where's the Mathematics?

Children may use various strategies for determining the values of their designs. To figure out the value when a hexagon equals 1, children might take apart the blocks in their design and put them together to form hexagons. If there are any leftover blocks, children might place them on a hexagon to see what fractional part of the block they cover. They could then count the number of whole hexagons they have and add the fractional value to this.

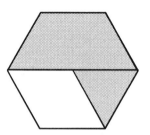

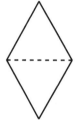

Together, a trapezoid and a triangle are ⅔ of a hexagon.

When the trapezoid or parallelogram has been assigned the value of 1, children might cover the blocks in their design with as many trapezoids or parallelograms as possible, count how many they have used for covering, and then figure any fractional parts formed by any uncovered blocks.

Other children might count the number of small triangles that could be used to cover their designs and figure out the total value by dividing the number of triangles by six if the hexagon is 1, by three if the trapezoid is 1, and by two if the parallelogram is 1.

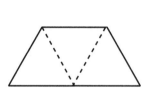

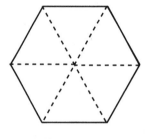

6 triangles   3 triangles   2 triangles

Children who have made designs containing repeating patterns may figure the value of only a part of their design and multiply to get the value of the total design. In the example below, the total value of the labeled pieces is 8; therefore, the value of the total design is 3 x 8, or 24.

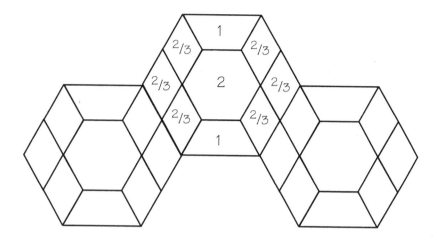

In looking for patterns in the values, children may notice that the value is a higher number if a smaller piece is assigned a value of 1. They may also notice that the value when a trapezoid equals 1 is twice as large as when the hexagon equals 1, and that the value when a parallelogram equals 1 is three times as large as when the hexagon equals 1. For example, if children find that the value of their design is 8⅔ when the hexagon equals 1, they should find that the value is 2 x 8⅔, or 17⅓ when the hexagon equals 1, and 3 x 8⅔, or 26 when the parallelogram equals 1. Some children may be able to extend this pattern to predict that if the green triangle were assigned the value of 1, the value of the design would be six times the value when the hexagon equals 1 (6 x 8⅔, or 52).

Some children may recognize that in finding the "values" of their designs, they are actually finding area using different sized measurement units. This may help them to understand that measurements are relative to some designated unit of measurement, and that that unit may sometimes be arbitrarily determined.

PATTERN BLOCK SHAPES

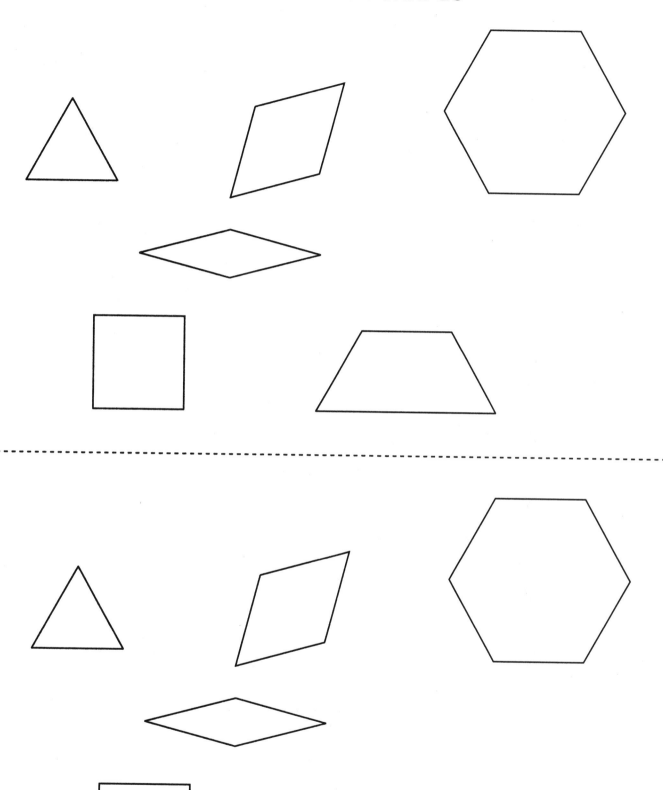

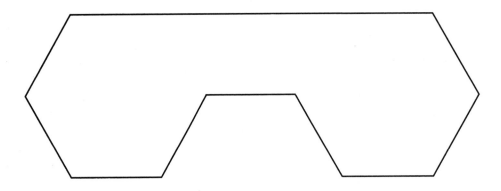

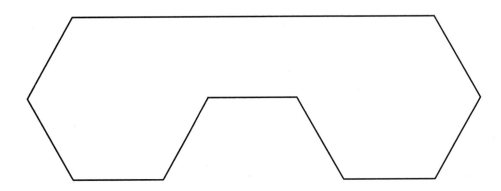

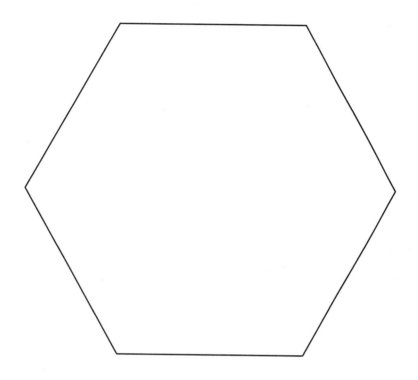

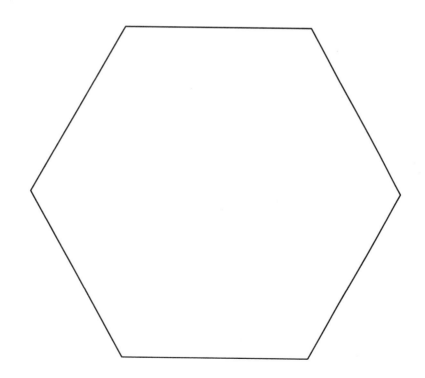

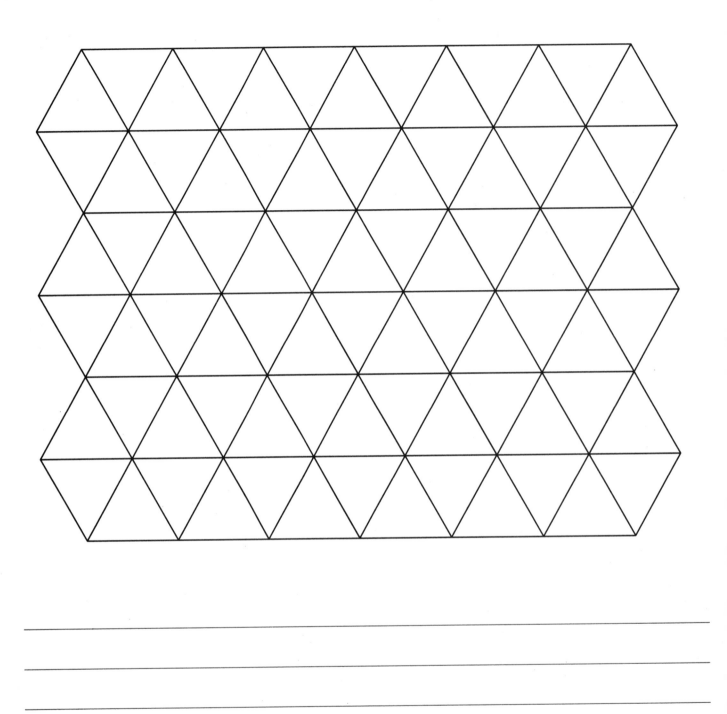

PATTERN BLOCK TRACING AND
WRITING PAPER